CORK HURLING

with Denis Hurley

www.**HERO**BOOKS.digital

HERO BOOKS

PUBLISHED BY HERO BOOKS
1 WOODVILLE GREEN
LUCAN
CO. DUBLIN
IRELAND

Hero Books is an imprint of Umbrella Publishing
First Published 2022
Copyright © Denis Hurley 2022
All rights reserved

A CIP record for this book is available from the British Library

ISBN 9781910827451

Cover design and formatting: jessica@viitaladesign.com
Ebook formatting: www.ebooklaunch.com
Photographs: Sportsfile

★ DEDICATION ★

To all those who wore the Cork jersey – and those
whose dreams they were living

★ CONTENTS ★

★ ACKNOWLEDGEMENTS ★

FIRST OF ALL, thanks to Liam Hayes of Hero Books. Having worked with Liam for Larry Tompkins' autobiography in 2019 and '20, I was delighted when he got in touch with the offer to do the Cork version of *Game of my Life*, which is proving to be an essential series of books. Liam's patience as circumstances forced me to delay the publication date of this book was greatly appreciated and, hopefully, there is enough credit in the bank with him that he will work with me again.

The 25 former Cork hurlers I spoke with are the real authors; the words are theirs and I am merely a stenographer. Some Cork stars have brought out their own autobiographies, while Adrian Russell's superb 2019 book *The Double* also featured great insights and so, rather than rehashing those publications, I tried to get fresh perspectives as much as possible. Equally, the current squad was avoided as, hopefully, the game of their lives is still to be played in a successful All-Ireland final in Croke Park.

Each of the players interviewed presented their own unique observations and memories, with the stories then brought together to provide a narrative covering more than half a century of Cork hurling history. Thanks to all of them, who willingly gave their time and reminiscences.

A couple of themes emerged as the interviews were ticked off. As will become clear, Fr Michael O'Brien – 'the Canon' – was a big character who played such a key role in the lives and careers of the players who came under his tutelage. As well as that, you realise that the Cork players, these warriors carrying out great deeds in red and white, were all influenced by those immediately before them, scarcely able to believe they were sharing a dressing-room with such famous names.

As Shane O'Neill – who had to repeat his contribution after my long-serving voice recorder finally made a break for freedom after 14 years, with his audio file still on it – says, they happen to be inside the wire in battle garb, but they are ultimately still fans themselves. None of them ever took the Cork jersey as anything less than a privilege.

My job is a lucky one – I am in a position where I can make contact with people who are heroes and ask them the questions I always wondered about. When my father Jim brought me to Cork games as a child – commencing with that marvellous 'double' summer of 1990 – he was my sounding board for those questions and generally had the right answers, or at least sound theories. I will be forever grateful for being given the opportunity to be present on so many great days for Cork, as well as those that were of the 'character-building' variety.

Those experiences – and the stream of questions – ultimately led me on the journalistic path that I took, aided by the love of reading and writing fostered by my mother Gretta. It is a source of sadness that a diagnosis of dementia at an obscenely young age means that she cannot enjoy this book, but I hope that she would be proud of it.

I love her, my father, siblings Susan, Lorna and James, brothers-in-law Cathal and Joe, soon-to-be-sister-in-law Ruth, and nieces Amelia, Fiadh and Maggie.

Because I am an Irish male, asking for assistance is not something that comes naturally but I am blessed to have a wide circle of friends in the Venn diagram of GAA and journalism. As I didn't explicitly request help, they may have been unaware of the important role they played in helping me reach the end of the project but, in various ways and in no particular order, a sincere thank you to Fintan O'Toole, Paul Dollery, John Horgan, Eoghan Cormican, Lisa Lawlor, Kieran McCarthy, Finbarr McCarthy, Tracey Kennedy, Joseph Blake, John Coleman, Patrick Mulcahy, Éanna Martin, Jamie Wall, David Sheehan, John Roycroft, Mary White and Robert O'Shea. Special mention must also be made of John McHale and Eamonn Murphy, editor and deputy editor respectively in the sports department at *The Echo*, a paper I am proud to work for.

Closer to home, I have two other bosses who are even more demanding. Quite a lot of this book was written while sitting outside the room of my elder son Johnny as he manfully battled against sleep; another chunk was done in the early mornings as his younger brother Aaron scuttled around the kitchen in his walker. There were even a couple of occasions – as Seánie McGrath in particular can vouch for – where the pair of them tried to help me conduct the player interviews.

Hopefully, when they are old enough, they can read this book and be inspired to great feats themselves. I will be proud of them whatever path life takes them down.

I love them and their mother, my wife Jessica – my bouts of parenting pale in comparison to the endless, tireless time she puts in. Jess allows me the time to indulge in my passions, but she is my greatest one. Hopefully the end product represents the support I have received.

Denis Hurley
January 2022

GERALD McCARTHY

CORK 3-9   KILKENNY 1-10
All-Ireland SHC Final
Croke Park
SEPTEMBER 4, 1966

Gerald McCarthy (on the right of the front row) with the Cork team that defeated Wexford in the 1976 All-Ireland final, 10 years after he captained his county in the winning final against Kilkenny.

★ **CORK:** P Barry; P Doolan, T O'Donoghue, D Murphy; T Connolly, J O'Sullivan, P Fitzgerald; J McCarthy (0-2), M Waters; S Barry (0-4), J O'Halloran, **G McCarthy** (0-1); C McCarthy (0-1), C Sheehan (3-0), J Bennett (0-1).

★ **KILKENNY:** O Walsh; P Henderson, J Lynch, J Treacy; S Cleere, T Carroll, M Coogan; P Moran, J Teehan (0-1); E Keher (0-7), C Dunne, S Buckley (0-1); J Dunphy (0-1), P Dillon, T Walsh (1-0). Sub: T Murphy for Dillon.

THE ACTION

CORK HADN'T WON the All-Ireland since 1954 (though the 1903-19 drought was longer) and had only won one Munster title in the interim, in 1956, but a young team had stormed through Munster and weren't fazed by the size of the task in front of them.

To commemorate the 50th anniversary of the 1916 Rising, 500 survivors of the insurrection were special guests of the GAA and, prior to the national anthem, the Artane Boys Band played *Oró Sé Do Bheatha 'Bhaile*.

Cork might have had an early goal but Charlie McCarthy was denied by Ollie Walsh and, with the wind behind them, Kilkenny had moved three points ahead when Eddie Keher pointed a free in the 13th minute. Their lead was 0-5 to 0-1, when Colm Sheehan scored the first of his three goals after good work from Jerry O'Sullivan and Seánie Barry.

While Kilkenny responded to lead by 0-7 to 1-2 by half-time, Cork were well in the game and a good point by captain Gerald McCarthy on the restart was followed by a Barry free after Sheehan had been fouled.

Keher did put Kilkenny back in front in the eighth minute of the second-half but Sheehan's second goal, from a Charlie McCarthy pass, put Cork into a lead that they would not lose. Barry's subsequent point made it 2-5 to 0-8.

The gap was narrowed to a single point again thanks to scores from Keher and Joe Dunphy, but Cork's third goal soon materialised. John O'Halloran was the architect, coming in from the right, and it seemed like his delivery might have gone all the way in but it was later revealed that Sheehan got a touch for his hat-trick.

That made it 3-5 to 0-10, and two long-range Justin McCarthy points sandwiched one by Barry to leave Cork seven in front. Tom Walsh did pull a goal back for Kilkenny in the 59th minute, but John Bennett pointed for Cork at the death.

Later that year, Cork would add the All-Ireland under-21 title, beating Wexford after the final went to two replays. Gerald McCarthy also skippered that side, creating a unique record that would never be equalled.

★★★★★

66

MY FATHER BROUGHT me to the All-Ireland final in 1956… Cork against Wexford. It was my first time in Croke Park and that really stirred something inside me. Christy Ring was going for nine All-Ireland medals, a record, and unfortunately Cork lost but the memories of that experience really sunk into my head – Art Foley's famous save from Ring, Nicky Rackard's goal… just the whole atmosphere. I would never have even dreamed that only 10 years later, I would play in an All-Ireland final, and captain Cork!

We lived on Bandon Road and I always had a hurley in my hand, even though it was all houses and a busy road. There was a gable end of a house with a chimney stack sticking out and there was an area about 20 yards wide that I used as a target.

My father played with Lough Rovers and I used to go to all of their games, so I had a good taste for hurling from a young age. He never pushed me to play for Lough Rovers but other people in the club used to say I was too good to play for them, and that I'd be better off going to the Barrs!

The Barrs underage team that I played on was a very good one, though at the time you couldn't call a juvenile team after the senior club. At under-13, it was Ard na Croithe, under-14 was St Brendan's, and the under-15 team was Greenmount. Hurling was our whole lives.

I played two years at minor level for Cork, in hurling and football. I was handy at the football and I enjoyed it, but hurling was my favourite game. The inter-county under-21 grade began in 1964, my first year out of minor, and so I played for Cork in the first three years of the competition, though we didn't get out of Munster in '64 or '65.

The call for the senior team came in 1964, too – though it almost ended up being my sole involvement. Cork were playing Wexford in the National League semi-final in Croke Park and I was named as a sub.

At the time, you'd travel up in taxis – all the Barrs fellas in one car, the Glen fellas in another, and so on. We decided to go into Dublin to see a picture and Tough (Jim Barry, our trainer) had warned us to be back by half past ten. When we came out of the cinema, it was a small bit late but Johnny Russell, God be good to him, was driving our car and he said he knew a short-cut through the Phoenix Park.

Of course, having gone up through it, the gate was locked when we reached the other side and we had to go back out and all the way around. When we got into the hotel, Tough was waiting at the bottom of the stairs and gave out mad to the older fellas. I stood at the back, trying to stay out of the way, but he pointed straight at me and said, 'As for you... this is your last time ever travelling with the Cork team!' I was rooming with Mick Archer and I could hardly sleep that night with the worry.

The following morning at breakfast, Tough came up to the table. 'I want to apologise to you,' he said. 'I thought you were the taxi driver!' I was a new face and he hadn't properly recognised me – you can imagine my relief!

Thankfully, I came on the next day. To be asked to wear the Cork senior jersey at the age of 18 and a half was great.

The Barrs won the county in 1965. We had a good mix of older players and younger guys coming up. I was surprised when I was told that I was being nominated as captain. Peter Doolan would have been a far more experienced player than I was, but that's just how it happened at the AGM. I was startled, but I took it and I was honoured. I didn't feel any extra pressure – I think people accepted that I was younger.

Cork hadn't won the All-Ireland since 1954. I had gone to a lot of the matches in between and I can remember defeat after defeat – we weren't even winning Munster Championships. We were getting beaten good by Tipperary every year and it kind of left a mark alright.

Tipp were knocked out early in 1966... destroyed by Limerick in the Athletic Grounds in a quarter-final, and that just opened it up for everyone else. I came on as a sub in the Munster quarter-final, when we drew with Clare, and kept my place for the reply and then the semi-final win over Limerick in Killarney.

We had Waterford in the Munster final and they were handy at the time; they still had quite a few from their All-Ireland winning team, but we beat them too. We were underdogs in practically every game and that definitely helped us big-time.

From midfield up, you have eight positions and four of those were filled by under-21s – Justin in midfield, Seánie Barry right half-forward, I was left half-forward and Charlie Mac was in the corner. That's a lot, in a forward line especially, but the way we approached it was… there was nothing to lose.

You're out there, trying to make a name for yourself. There are times like that when you just need to give youth its chance and I think that's something we're seeing with the current Cork side, who got to the 2021 All-Ireland final with a very young team.

Midfield would have been my preferred position, but I did play quite a bit at wing-forward. I played wing-back in one All-Ireland final and centre-forward in another.

I was working in McCarthy Stone-Cutters in White St at the time. That was my trade, like my father and grandfather before me, but it wasn't our family business; they were different McCarthys. It was in the late 1970s that I started my own business in a small shop on Barrack St, stone-cutting and making trophies.

In 1966, Liam MacCarthy was the trophy I was keen on, but Kilkenny were raging-hot favourites, no doubt about it. Still, we were building confidence along the way. We had won a few championship matches and that gives you belief – we were willing to have a go at it. We knew we were very good and we weren't overawed by them. We also had a very experienced team – Peter Doolan, Tom O'Donoghue, Jerry O'Sullivan, Denis Murphy, Tony Connolly, John O'Halloran and Paddy Fitzgerald, father of Ger. John Bennett had come out of retirement that year, so we had a good mix. Another thing in our favour was the following that we had. It was unbelievable.

It was a first final for all of us and you'd expect that we'd be nervous. We stayed out in the West County Hotel in Chapelizod and, on the Sunday morning, when we got on the coach to Croke Park, all of a sudden, a sing-song started and, all the way to Croke Park, we never stopped! They were all Rebel songs… *And we're all off to Dublin in the green, in the green/Where the helmets glisten in the sun.*

It was brilliant and it relaxed everybody, the atmosphere was great. Whoever started it, I don't know… he was a brave man but it worked!

We were as fit as we were going to be, there's no doubt about that. We didn't have to be killing ourselves training for the final at all. Jim Barry was a seasoned trainer and he knew his stuff. The last thing that he'd have wanted would be that we'd all be 'flahed' out on the Sunday. He certainly prepared us well.

There was no introducing the players to the President or anything – as captain, all I had to do was go up for the toss. Even when Kilkenny started well, we never panicked. For Colm Sheehan to score three goals in an All-Ireland final was a superb achievement, and those goals were the difference in the end.

When it was over, the crowd swarmed on to the field, the whole place was covered in red and white! I was very inexperienced in giving speeches. Tony O'Shaughnessy was a selector and he had said to me during the week that I should have something ready. I prepared a few words – I got a bit of help! – and I gave it to Tony.

He had it in his pocket, but trying to find him wasn't easy with all of the people… I could hardly move!

What a night we had. My girlfriend at the time, Mary – my wife now – was there with me. At that time, you daren't bring a woman into the Cork set-up! But they were all there that night and it was a change forever! The homecoming was incredible. When we came around Paddy Barry's Corner - the corner of Bridge St and McCurtain St, the bottom of St Patrick's Hill -and you could look all the way down, it was breathtaking. The only other thing I can compare with it is Ringy's funeral.

I won four more All-Irelands as a player and then one as trainer in 1990. They were all pleasing, but the first one is always the most special, and all the more so to win as captain.

I was captain of the Cork under-21s in 1966 as well and that team made it to the All-Ireland final against Wexford. Unfortunately, I was injured in the county football final when the Barrs played St Nicholas' – I was concussed and I couldn't play in the under-21 final in Nowlan Park, which ended in a draw. I went but I wasn't even an official sub or anything.

The replay was in Limerick; I was a sub that day and came in, and we drew again! I was fine for the third game, in Croke Park. We beat them well… it was a lovely way to round off the year.

99

TONY MAHER

NEW YORK 2-8 CORK 1-10
National League Final Second-Leg
(aggregate Cork 5-21 New York 6-16)
Gaelic Park
SEPTEMBER 20, 1970

President of the GAA Nickey Brennan in the company of Carol Ann Lennon, Director of Marketing, Vodafone, presents Tony Maher, a member of the hurling All Stars of 1971, with a commemorative medal to mark the 35th Anniversary of the All Star Awards scheme at a special celebration in Croke Park.

★ **NEW YORK:** H Condon; P O'Donoghue, J Maher, J O'Neill; M Reynolds, P Dowling, P Dwyer; J Firth, M Curtin (1-1); T Corbett (0-2), J Carney (0-4), D O'Brien (0-1); S Lakes, B Hennessy, P Kirby. Subs: J Foley for Kirby, B Kelleher for Carney.

★ **CORK:** P Barry; **T Maher**, P McDonnell, J Hordan; S Murphy, P Hegarty, C Roche; S Looney, G McCarthy (0-1); T Ryan (0-2), W Walsh (0-1), D Clifford (1-0); C McCarthy (0-6), R Cummins, E O'Brien. Subs: J O'Sullivan for G McCarthy, G McCarthy for O'Sullivan.

THE ACTION

VAL DORGAN OF *The Cork Examiner* painted a vivid picture in his report the day after the game. '*Now, still touched by the emotional impact, I say that I have never seen in 15 years of reporting, an hour so filled with tension and a climax so incredible. I frizzled in the 80-degree heat of the press box, convinced that the estimated 7,500 people and the players and, not least of all, the referee, were sitting on a slow fuse burning down to an explosion of over-wrought feeling.*'

Unfortunately, Dublin referee Clem Foley was to suffer a rough fate at the end, assaulted as he left the field. He would require the insertion of a steel plate into his jaw and would be out of work for 14 weeks as he recovered. New York and Cork had been due to meet again in the World Cup final a few weeks later back in Ireland but Central Council postponed that game for a week. Having travelled for the original date in the hope of a reversion, New York refused to play the re-fixture which led to the cancellation of the football World Cup against Kerry.

For Cork, defeat by fewer than three points meant that they were declared league champions, having won by 4-11 to 4-8 in the first-leg at Gaelic Park. Coupled with their All-Ireland final win over Kilkenny a fortnight previously, it resulted in the county's fourth league and championship double, and the first since 1953.

It was as hard-earned as any trophy in Cork's history. Within the opening 15 minutes, New York had wiped out Cork's three-point aggregate lead. While Gerald McCarthy excelled at midfield for Cork, the attack struggled in Gaelic Park's narrow confines, but there was a boost in the 20th minute as Donal Clifford struck for a goal. By half-time, the sides were level, 0-5 to 1-2, after a good Willie Walsh point.

They pushed on after half-time to move 1-6 to 0-6 in front, but a wonderful Mick Curtin goal for New York levelled the game and brought the tie back into the melting pot. While two Charlie McCarthy frees put Cork ahead again, Brendan Kelleher netted a 21-yard free for New York with four minutes left – though Cork protested that the ball had gone over the bar. Tom Corbett's point made it 2-7 to 1-8 and the game was in injury-time when Charlie McCarthy and Curtin pointed for their respective sides. McCarthy slotted Cork's final free at the death, ensuring a one-point defeat but a two-point overall cushion.

★★★★★

66

AFTER WINNING THE league final in 1970, we were meant to go out to New York.

The previous year, after beating us in the All-Ireland, Kilkenny went over there for what was called the World Cup... and New York beat them well. Taking the boxing prize-fight approach, New York were kind of saying that they were All-Ireland champions and, so, it was decided that the winners of the 'Home' league final would take them on for the league title.

The league final was usually played around the start of May, so that you'd be ready for the championship. Our final with Limerick was on May 3 and the New York final was to be over two legs, so Cork County Board looked for a postponement because the championship was coming up so quickly.

We won Munster again and then we went on and won the All-Ireland, so the matches in New York were fixed for the following two weekends. I think it was the Tuesday after the All-Ireland that we flew out. I worked as a dyer in Seafield Fabrics on Kinsale Road and there was no issue with getting the time off, even though it was a second trip out there that year – I had played for Munster in the Cardinal Cushing Games earlier in the season.

When I was growing up, I never believed that I'd be able to play for Cork, not at all. My whole ambition was just to go out and play hurling, and if you got on the Barrs senior team it would have been a marvellous achievement. When I was growing up, if the Barrs won the county they used to march up Bandon Road with the cup to Mok's pub.

Mrs Cregan – the mother of Denis, who went on to set up the Dino's chip shop chain – lived next door to us. She had a barrel and that would be lighting as they came up. Later on, if you were lucky enough to be on the team, you'd have the privilege of going upstairs in Mok's and holding the cup out the window!

I'm from Bandon Road, up by Fr O'Leary Hall – the heart of Barrs' territory. We all started playing down in the street leagues at the Lough. I played for McCurtain Villas... the team was run by a guy called Stevie Cotter. The matches would be on after Mass and there would be huge crowds there. They were great days. You'd be playing against these fellas who you'd go on to become teammates with – there were a few Nemo Rangers lads there too!

The first time we came together for the Barrs was at under-14. Then, if you can believe it, Gerald McCarthy and myself ran the under-14 team when we were under-16! We used to be always pucking around, down by the Lough or in Greenmount school, the field was known as 'the Dia'. We won the Dick Barrett Shield at under-15 level down in the Park. That was all ground hurling… you could only catch the ball in flight.

When we were playing minor, we had a very good team – Gerald Mac, Charlie Mac, Con Roche, Brian McKeon. We were six goals up against Blackrock at half-time in the county final, but they beat us! They had a big thing a few years ago, celebrating the 50th anniversary of that county win… Kevin Cummins of Blackrock would be slagging me about it whenever we meet him! We relaxed in the second-half – we were all starting to work at that stage and a lot of us had been on holidays down in Crosshaven the week before the match. We had no second-half performance!

At that time, you came out of minor and you played junior. You got toughened up… definitely. Nowadays, if you've a talented young fella, there's no way would he be allowed to play down junior and I think that's a lot of our problem in Cork at the moment.

I started playing with the Barrs seniors in 1965. They had been in the county final the year before and the Glen had annihilated them, so the Barrs selectors decided to get new fellas in and we won the county – it was a very young team, seven or eight of the fellas had played minor in the two or three years before that. It was the best thing to happen to me playing hurling… to win a county with your club was marvellous.

We had chances to win the county again in 1966, when the College beat us in the semi-final, and '67, when we lost to the Glen in the final… but we beat Imokilly in the 1968 final.

I had played minor for Cork and I was on the under-21 team in 1966 – well, I was on and off the team! There were two draws against Wexford in the final, before we won the third game. Then, after the 1968 county final, I was picked to play for Cork against Wexford in the Oireachtas Cup.

I was chosen at centre-back but I wasn't really bothered as I had played in nearly every position for the Barrs – fellas thought nothing of that. I was playing on a fella called Jack Berry and it was the first of a few times that we marked each other.

I did well enough and I kept my place after that. The man in charge was Jim O'Regan; he was originally from Kinsale and he was a schoolteacher out in Glasheen. He was a fierce tough man. Cork won the National League in 1969... the first time since '53. It was great for the likes of myself and other lads who hadn't been playing previously. There was great enthusiasm and to win a national title was brilliant.

We did very well in that year's Munster Championship; we beat Tipperary in the final, but then the All-Ireland final against Kilkenny is one we still talk about in terms of throwing it away. We were very disappointed, especially after winning the Oireachtas in 1968, and then the league and Munster. I marked Tommy Murphy that day. He was a priest, a very nice fella, and we had a good tussle. Obviously, Eddie Keher was the star of that Kilkenny team but the rest of the forwards made him. He could put the ball over the bar from anywhere... he'd find a bit of space and the likes of Pat Delaney, or later Kieran Purcell, would win it and give it to him.

In 1970, we bounced back well. We played Tipp in the league semi-final, a match and a half up in Thurles... we beat them by three points. Tipp had some great players; Noel O'Dwyer, who was a good friend of mine, Mick Roche, and Jimmy Doyle, who I'd become great pals with later on. But then we had Willie Walsh from Youghal coming through. He was a really tough player, and Joe Murphy from Passage, who sadly died at a young age. Tom Ryan from Inniscarra and Pat McDonnell... some great players. Simon Murphy from Blackrock... he could be brought on anywhere... a big, strong man. He was another who died relatively young.

We were going well in the Barrs and we had six on the Cork team – Gerald, Charlie, myself, Rochey and Charlie Cullinane, and Séamus Looney was coming through.

We beat Limerick well in the final in Croke Park – two league titles in-a-row after going so long without one! It was a great bunch of players and there was a strong unity. Paddy Barry was captain in 1970. He was a great goalkeeper... a great character. There was a great camaraderie there. We might go out the following week and play against each other for our clubs but, once we put on the Cork jersey, that was the end of it.

We hadn't trained since the All Ireland final and New York had some great players. They had Pat Kirby from Clare, who was an All-Ireland champion handballer, and Mick Morrissey from Wexford. There were Cork lads, too… Tom Corbett from the Glen, Pat Dowling from Sars and Bernie Murphy from Cloyne… as well as Brendan Hennessy from Kerry, a horse of a man.

The momentum had been with New York after beating Kilkenny in 1969, but Cork putting the match back from May to September might have broken that somewhat.

Gaelic Park was short and narrow, and we put black grease around our eyes for the glare. Clem Foley was a referee from Dublin and Central Council sent him over because there had been an incident a few years prior with a local ref. The first match took a while to settle but we won by 4-11 to 4-8, with Charlie Mac getting 2-5 for us. With only a goal in it, we knew that the second match would be a dog-fight and it certainly was… it was the toughest match I ever played in my life.

We actually lost the second-leg by a point, but won on aggregate by two. It was backs to the wall, there was no quarter asked or given. You just defended yourself as best you could and didn't let anybody blackguard you. There was no grass on the pitch and you can imagine what it was like playing on a dust-track… the ball could have bounced anywhere, and players just whipped and pulled and stood up for each other.

The crowd was hostile and Gaelic Park was like a cauldron.

You came out on the field and it was like you were in a bull-fighting arena. Given the circumstances, I thought the display the lads gave that day was outstanding. We all fought for each other – there was nobody given time to have a free shot at goal and there was no hand-passing that day!

If they had got a late goal, they would have won it. It felt like we were defending for about a quarter of an hour at the end. I don't think it would have devalued the All-Ireland if we had lost the league title, but it just showed how fellas were willing to stand up for themselves when the chips were down. We had built a team from 1968 and you could have made the case that we could have won three or four in-a-row but, that day in New York, there was one fella better than the other.

We had got to know Clem Foley because he did a bit of running with us when we trained in New York, but he didn't do anything out of the way in the matches. He sent off two fellas in the first game, but that was only a tea party in comparison to the second match! Unfortunately, the final whistle wasn't the end of it. Clem was coming off the field at the end and he was assaulted. Someone came at him from behind and gave him a dig in the eye and a dig in the jaw... breaking it.

As far as I can remember, there was a priest who came on to the field and he got Clem into the dressing-room. Connie Neenan, who was a great Barrs benefactor and after whom our grounds are named, worked with Waterford Glass in New York and it was he who helped Clem get in. And he later paid for him to get his jaw wired up and repaired.

The New York County Board was suspended for two years after that.

Tipperary won the All-Ireland in 1971 and that was another one that we could have won. I got an All Star that year and I became great friends with Jimmy Doyle when we went out to San Francisco on that tour.

In later years, when Tipperary were playing in Cork, Jimmy would come down on the train and come to my house for something to eat... and we'd go out to the Barrs clubhouse and he'd have a drink, and then we'd go down to the match. What stood out for me is you start with your club and you finish with your club.

We were great friends, and I made so many others from my time playing. I've so many wonderful memories but that day in New York will always stay with me.

BRIAN MURPHY

CORK 2-21 WEXFORD 4-11
All-Ireland SHC Final
Croke Park
SEPTEMBER 5, 1976

Cork captain Ray Cummins prepares to make his speech after being presented with the Liam MacCarthy Cup by GAA President Con Murphy in 1976. Also pictured are (from left) Cork County Board Chairman Donal O'Sullivan, Pat McDonnell, John Horgan, Martin O'Doherty, Charlie McCarthy, Martin Coleman, Denis Coughlan, Gerald McCarthy, Brian Murphy, Eamonn O'Donoghue, Sean O'Leary, John Allen and Mick Malone.

★ **CORK:** M Coleman; **B Murphy**, P McDonnell, M O'Doherty; PM Barry, J Crowley, D Coughlan; G McCarthy, P Moylan (0-10); M Malone (0-1), B Cummins, J Barry-Murphy (0-4); C McCarthy (1-3), R Cummins (1-2), S O'Leary (0-1). Subs: E O'Donoghue for O'Leary, J Horgan for Barry.

★ **WEXFORD:** J Nolan; T O'Connor, W Murphy, J Prendergast; L Bennett, M Jacob, C Doran; N Buggy (0-5), B Rowsome; J Murphy, M Quigley (2-1), J Quigley (0-1); M Butler (1-4), T Doran (1-0), C Keogh. Subs: D Rowsome for Keogh, M Casey for B Rowsome.

THE ACTION

CORK JOINED TIPPERARY at the top of the roll of honour with their 22nd All-Ireland title, winning by four points despite allowing Wexford an eight-point head-start.

Vital in the game going Cork's way were two important positional switches involving players who were adding themselves to the list of those to have claimed senior hurling and football medals – Brian Murphy's move to full-back helped to curtail a previously rampant Tony Doran, while Wexford centre-back Mick Jacob, who had cut a swathe up to then against a variety of Cork centre-forwards, was finally bested by Jimmy Barry-Murphy in the last 10 minutes or so. Denis Coughlan also made himself a dual winner.

After Mick Butler's free gave Wexford the lead and Ned Buggy doubled it, they had a fifth-minute goal as Martin Quigley doubled to the net, having been set up by Doran. A minute later, the same player was on hand to fire home after Martin Coleman had saved from Doran and, though Pat Moylan did have Cork's opening point in the eighth minute, Butler replied to make it 2-3 to 0-1 for Wexford.

Cork, without a title since 1970, were not perturbed and reeled off seven points in-a-row to cut the gap to just one – the inspirational Moylan and captain Ray Cummins leading the way. While Wexford pushed on again, Cork were level five minutes before half-time as Jimmy Barry-Murphy set up Cummins for a kicked goal and Seánie O'Leary, starting despite carrying an injury, put them ahead for the first time.

Charlie McCarthy put them two ahead but back Wexford came, with points from Buggy and John Quigley levelling by half-time, 2-8 to 1-11, before Doran put them in front with a goal on the resumption. The third quarter was an arm wrestle: after a Moylan point, Charlie McCarthy's goal gave Cork the lead once more. While Martin Quigley equalised, Cork moved two ahead only for Butler to net Wexford's fourth goal. With Cork wasting chances, it seemed like it might be the Model County's day.

The personnel movements gave Cork some balance though and a two-point deficit was cleared thanks to Moylan and Barry-Murphy, before the latter put them in front for a lead they would hold for the remainder. Moylan had the final say with his tenth point.

★★★★★

"

PLAYING IN MY first All-Ireland senior final in 1972 was memorable, even though we lost to Kilkenny, who produced a great comeback. Coming back to win in 1976 against Wexford, the first-leg of the three in-a-row, is a treasured memory.

Nowadays, my native club Nemo Rangers are premier senior in football and junior A in hurling, but at that time, before we won our first senior football title, we were going well in hurling, too. The club won the county minor hurling title in 1970 – the late Séamus Coughlan, who went on to win the senior football All-Ireland with Cork in 1973, was on that team with me.

Then we won the county Intermediate Hurling Championship in 1971 and were senior for a few years and made it to a semi-final – we were beaten by only a few points by Blackrock, who had a very good team at that time. There were a lot of dual players involved. I loved playing both and obviously Nemo went on to become very strong in football in the 1970s, but if it came down to it, I probably had a slight preference for hurling.

I came on to both Cork senior panels around the same time, in 1971 or so. The goal of every young fella at the time was to get to play with the Cork senior hurling team and I was lucky enough to come in and play with these fellas that I had looked up to when I was growing up. It was a golden era for Cork at underage level. There was success at minor and under-21 in football and hurling, and the colleges were going well too, which fed into that.

I had been stationed as a garda in Kilkenny since 1971, so I had to commute.

The training nowadays is way different to what it was then, but once the championship was on the horizon, I was on the road from Kilkenny to Cork a lot. There was no motorway back then, but I didn't really mind the travelling that much at that time. As the years went on, it did become harder, especially after getting married and having kids.

For All-Ireland semi-finals and finals, I used to make my own way up to Dublin and meet the team up there. Leading up to a game, I'd try to relax and not be over-anxious. You'd be nervous enough on the day itself, but that was a good sign – if you weren't nervous, you mightn't have the right attitude!

Once I got the first touch of the ball, I was able to settle.

Cork had won the hurling All-Ireland in 1970, then Tipperary won in '71 and we were back in the All-Ireland final in '72... an 80-minute final. People say that it was a great game – and it might have been for the neutral! – but from a Cork point of view, it wasn't a good result. Cork were nine points up with about 16 or 17 minutes to go... and were beaten by seven, which was an awful turnaround.

After a defeat like that, you were fairly down because there was no guarantee that you'd get back the following year – and we didn't, as it happened, because Limerick won the next two Munster Championships. But, luckily enough for me, the Cork footballers made it to the All-Ireland final in 1973 and I was part of that team! There were a lot of fellas on that team that I admired from a club point of view and a county point of view, so it was great to get in there.

The Cork hurlers were beaten by Galway in the All-Ireland semi-final in 1975. Cork had a very good team but we had a very bad start; we conceded three goals in the first few minutes and it was catch-up after that. Even though we got close, Galway held on and beat us. What made it worse for us looking on was that Galway disappointed in the final against Kilkenny. Then, after we won the three in-a-row, the same thing happened in 1979 – Galway beat us to stop us going for four, but Kilkenny beat them in the final!

After 1975, we came back to win Munster in 1976, though we were very lucky to get over Tipperary in the semi-final – we won by 4-10 to 2-15 and one of the reasons we won was Martin Coleman making a couple of great saves. After one of them, I saw him making the sign of the cross and I remember asking him afterwards, what that was all about – he said he hadn't seen the ball at all! For us, it was great to be back in the final and have a chance to make up for 1972.

Certainly, having been there already was a help. Even in 2021, from a Cork point of view, you had 13 players going out against Limerick who had never played in an All-Ireland final before and that does make a difference. There were lots of reasons that they didn't play to their potential but having only two players who had played in an All-Ireland before then had to have a bearing on the match, given that all of the Limerick team had been there in the couple of years beforehand.

The first Leinster final I went to was in 1976, when Wexford were playing Kilkenny, who were going for three in-a -row and had a very good team. Wexford hammered them and, as there was only one semi-final in those days, it was the Leinster champions' turn to play Galway – Wexford eventually came through after a replay in the new Páirc Uí Chaoimh. We knew that the All-Ireland final was going to be a big battle.

Like in 1975 against Galway, we started quite poorly and Wexford got two goals and a couple of points early on, so they went eight points up within a few minutes. It would be crossing your mind that things might go the same as against Galway, but Cork were very good up front and we worked our way back into the game and were level at half-time.

Gerald McCarthy and Pat Moylan formed a very good midfield partnership, and Pat was on the frees that day... he was excellent. Nowadays, you see players knock frees over from 120 yards but, back then, even to score a '65' was a big thing... and Pat scored some great frees. On the other side, Wexford missed some frees, particularly towards the end, and they were costly for them. Ray Cummins was one of the greatest forwards of all time and he kicked a goal and a point for Cork that day. And Charlie McCarthy got a goal that would be regarded as fantastic even in today's game.

I always preferred playing corner-back. I did play full-back for the footballers and the hurlers, but I never liked the position, really. I was certainly glad that it was Pat McDonnell who was full-back rather than myself in 1976, as he was on Tony Doran, who was one of the best forwards around.

I did end up going on Tony towards the end and I was involved in a controversial incident with him. Tony would be inclined to go straight rather than go around you, and when he did that with me, we both ended up on the ground.

There was a bit of debate as to whether it should be a free in and I was kind of anxious but the referee, Paddy Johnson – who was from Kilkenny – came along and, in his wisdom, decided to throw the ball in. I knew Paddy and all of his umpires and one of them, Kevin Byrne, says to me that Cork needed him to win an All-Ireland that year as Paddy came into him and asked what the decision should be... and he said a throw-in!

We had good people on the line. Kevin Kehilly was training the team and we were very fit. Fr Bertie Troy was the coach and Frank Murphy, Jimmy Brohan,

Denis Murphy and Christy Ring were the selectors. Christy was such a fantastic player and people would nearly be in awe of him, but he was a great hurling brain to have around and they say he was responsible for one of the most important moves that day. Mick Jacob was having a great game at centre-back for Wexford, but Ringy said that he was tiring and to get Jimmy Barry-Murphy in on him.

Jimmy had been having a quiet game by his standards up to then, but he had a great finish and that was one of the reasons that we won. As well as that, John Horgan, God rest him, was brought on and he had a stormer.

The game went to and fro. We had come back level by half-time after the slow start and so we were in a far better position than Wexford, who were surely wondering how they let a lead of eight points go. In fairness to them, they kept us under pressure in the second-half and they were two points up with 10 minutes to go, but they missed an easy free to go three ahead.

Then Cork made the move, with Jimmy coming out, and we finished the better team.

There was one notable thing about that match, which I hadn't come across before. One of the Wexford lads, John Quigley – a fine player, in fairness – was a great man for talking on the field, and he wouldn't be complimenting you!

I hadn't experienced that before then. Wexford had some outstanding players, really – they were unfortunate not to win an All-Ireland – but we just got over the line.

Winning the three in-a-row was a special achievement.

We had fellas that came in in 1977 – Tom Cashman, Dermot McCurtain and Tim Crowley – and they were huge additions, even though they were quite young. Martin Coleman probably doesn't get the credit due to him, but he made some fantastic saves, especially the one from Christy Keogh in 1977. Poor Christy has passed away since – like quite a few of the players from those times – but I was supposed to be marking him, so I was extra relieved that Martin made the block!

MARTIN COLEMAN

CORK 1-17   WEXFORD 3-8
All-Ireland SHC Final
Croke Park
SEPTEMBER 4, 1977

Martin Coleman (centre in white) celebrates Cork's 1976 All-Ireland final win, but it was a second victory over Wexford in 1977 which was the 'Game of his Life'.

★ **CORK: M Coleman**; B Murphy, M O'Doherty, J Horgan; D McCurtain, J Crowley, D Coughlan; T Crowley, T Cashman (0-1); M Malone, G McCarthy (0-6), J Barry-Murphy (0-2); C McCarthy (0-5), R Cummins (0-1), S O'Leary (1-2). Subs: P Moylan for Malone, T Murphy for G McCarthy.

★ **WEXFORD:** J Nolan; T O'Connor, W Murphy, J Prendergast; L Bennett, M Jacob, C Doran; D Bernie, E Buggy (1-4); C Keogh (0-1), M Quigley, M Butler (1-2); J Quigley (0-1), T Doran (1-0), J Murphy. Subs: J Russell for Prendergast, M Casey for Murphy, E Walsh for Bernie.

THE ACTION

WHEN CORK PARADED around the pitch beforehand, there were only 14 players present – Seánie O'Leary had been struck on the nose by a flying sliothar in the pre-match puckaround. Legend has it that Christy Ring, then a selector, told him that he didn't play hurling with his nose and that he'd be fine! Patched up and ready to play, the Youghal man would contribute 1-2.

While Mick Butler had the game's opening score for Wexford, it was the only time they led in the whole match. With Tom Cashman on song at midfield and the switch of Gerald McCarthy to centre-forward paying off for Cork as he nullified the great Mick Jacob, Cork ensured a regular supply to their full-forward line.

After 16 minutes Cork led by 0-7 to 0-3 and could have been further ahead, but Wexford gave themselves a lifeline as Tony Doran scored a goal and the half-time scoreline of 0-9 to 1-4 in Cork's favour was far from unmanageable for the Model County. Early in the second-half, Gerald McCarthy's dead-ball prowess helped Cork to push on again but, once more, a goal brought Wexford right back into the game, with Ned Buggy crashing home a 21-yard free.

It brought them back to within a point, 0-12 to 2-5, but Cork responded in the style of champions, producing a dominant 10-minute spell that was ultimately to prove to be the winning of the game. After O'Leary went close to a goal, foiled by goalkeeper John Nolan, Ray Cummins' point extended the lead, before O'Leary did find the net, palming the ball home after catching Gerald McCarthy's long delivery.

Four more points – two superlative Charlie McCarthy efforts and one each from Gerald McCarthy and Jimmy Barry-Murphy – answered only by one from Wexford's Christy Keogh, left Cork eight ahead and coasting, so much so that chances to extend the lead were wasted.

They didn't look to be costly at first, but then Wexford responded with a third goal as Mick Butler netted following a blocked Buggy free. Two frees from Buggy had the margin down to just three, and Cork were wavering. Wexford sensed an unlikely revival and they were almost level as Jacob intercepted a clearance and found Keogh just inside the '21'. He went for goal, but Coleman was equal to the effort.

★★★★★

66

WEXFORD DIDN'T GET the whirlwind start they had got the year before. We were all going well and we were up four points but then, all of a sudden, Wexford got a goal and a point and it was level pegging again.

We were a point or two ahead at half-time, a good position, but in the second-half then we went into overdrive mode and moved eight ahead. I asked the umpire how long was left and he said, 'It's all over, Coleman… there's around eight or nine minutes left'. I didn't trust him at all as it was my seventh or eighth final against Wexford across all grades, and they'd always come back at you.

Next thing, Ned Buggy got a '21'… BANG… GOAL!

Then they got two frees and there were only three points in it. Again, I asked the umpire, 'How much time is left… is it over?'

He said, 'There's three minutes, and ye're in trouble, buddy! I tell ya Coleman, they'll be the three longest minutes you'll ever play in your life… the best of luck to you!'

I played my first match for Cork in 1970, an All-Ireland semi-final against London, after two nights' training!

I was on the under-21 team at the time, but I was up in Galway on holidays and on the Friday evening my brother Donal rang me and said, 'You'd better come home, you're on the panel for the match on Sunday week'. I said to him that the under-21s weren't playing, but he said that, no, it was the senior panel. John Mitchell had been the sub goalkeeper; he used to play for UCC, but there was some falling-out and he had left the panel.

They drafted me in and I trained Tuesday and Wednesday night and then, because Paddy Barry had injured his hand playing football, I was playing on the Sunday. He was back for the final alright… and I was a sub.

When you're young and innocent, you take the bull by the horns and you're willing to face anything. I had three or four years on the sideline after that; the next time I played was down in Walsh Park in 1974 when Barry was put off against Waterford and I was brought on.

I had youth on my side and Ballinhassig were going well; we were climbing out of the junior ranks, and Carrigdhoun – the south-east divisional side – had a good period around then, too. That kind of kept me going and kept me in the public eye, which was very important for a fella from a country club at the time. Glen Rovers, Blackrock and the Barrs were dominating at the time, so their fellas got a lot of exposure… it was up to the other fellas then to try to step up to the mark.

Cork were after winning four under-21 titles in-a-row and I had been involved in two, 1970 and '71. Bernard Hurley from Blackrock had been in goal for the previous two.

That day down in Waterford, I was thrown in at half-time.

Jack Barrett said to me, 'Don't let me down!'

And I replied, 'Well I've nowhere else to go, I suppose!' It's better in a way just to have it like that, because you don't have too much time to think about it. You're waiting four years for an opportunity like that and, all of a sudden, it's sprung on you and you think to yourself… *Well, sink or f***ing swim now!*

We were beaten by a couple of points that day, but I played well – I'd say I was the only happy Corkman coming out of Walsh Park that day! I had always wanted to play in the Munster Senior Championship for Cork and, if I never again pucked a ball, at least I'd be able to say I did that. That's every young fella's dream when he catches a hurley – the medals come after, but to play your first proper senior game for your county is something special. There's nothing that can buy it or come near it afterwards… maybe winning your first All-Ireland, but you're more mature by that stage and more settled.

Barry was suspended for a couple of months and I was given a chance as the starter. Jim Power from the Barrs was the sub to me for a while but then Paddy came back for a couple of matches and he was the sub. We were above in Thurles one day – we had a bit of a racket with Tipp – and I played well, and Paddy came up to me afterwards. 'The best of luck to you, Martin,' he said. 'I don't think I'll get the smell of it again from you. I hope you win a few All-Irelands.'

I thought it was nice from him… and he was only 32 or 33, which wasn't that old and still isn't for a goalkeeper. He had the bottle to come up and wish me the best of luck, which I respected.

We won Munster in 1975, but Galway caught us in the All-Ireland semi-final – they got three goals in the first 10 minutes. We came back at them, but we gave away a bad goal again after that. Galway had to beat us sometime in the championship, I suppose – we were just unlucky to be the Cork team that lost to them!

It wasn't hugely difficult to put an early concession like that behind you, as you had time to come back. You'd be rattled, definitely – especially in Croke Park, you'd be saying that this is where you wanted to play, and the first thing you're having to do is to take the ball out of the net. But you have to accept that there are going to be goals scored against you.

I had a great Munster final that year against Limerick. I kept a clean sheet, but that won't happen every day, as the Galway match proved!

I remember going up on the train to the 1976 final – back then, there was no special train or anything, so you were mingling with the supporters. Din Joe Buckley, the Lord have mercy on him, called me over. He used to play for Cork in the 1940s and he said, 'Martin, sit down there. The best of luck tomorrow and I hope you beat Dave Creedon's record'.

I asked him what that was and he said, 'He only let in one goal in three All-Irelands'. I said thanks to him and that I appreciated it coming from a Glen Rovers man but, the following day, I remember looking up at the scoreboard after nine minutes and there were two goals gone in. I was thinking… *Feck you Din Joe, anyway!* We came back to win it though, the first of the three in-a-row.

Christy Ring was a selector. He wasn't a great man to speak in the dressing-room or in a meeting, but he'd go around to every individual player. Being a goalie, I used to have great chats with him.

He'd never call you by your first name. It was always… 'Coleman! We have to beat these fellas so you'll need to be on your toes on Sunday!'

You'd go home and you wouldn't be able to sleep, for fear of letting him down – he hated the thought of Cork being, 'deprived of an All-Ireland'… as he put it. He was the epitome of the Glen attitude – when the Glen are with you, they're with you one hundred and ten percent. I went out to the Glen the week after the 1977 final and I got a standing ovation. We weren't allowed to put our hands in our pockets that night. You felt at home with them.

At another club, you might get one pint off them, but the Glen treated us royally. They might kill you on the field of play in the county championship but, as regards Cork, they were A1.

Ringy would come up and just grab you... 'This is it now, boy! This is it! This is it!' His other line was... 'Get the other crowd thinking!'

We all rose our games that day for Ringy and revenge for 1956, when Wexford had beaten Cork to deny him a ninth All-Ireland. Cork hurling is built on tradition and it's a powerful one.

There was a goodwill about Cork hurling at that time. We were like a club team and I can't recall any arguments in the dressing-room or anything like that. It didn't make any difference who you were togging out alongside, everyone was pulling together for Cork. For instance, Ray Cummins called to me a while back and, while you mightn't see a fella like that for 10 years, you can just pick up again where you left off. We were all singing off the one hymn-sheet.

We could have won five in-a-row as easily as three in-a-row – you always feel you should have won more, and you're reliving various different things and saying that we could have done this or done that. When I got involved afterwards as a selector, I noticed that there would be players forming cliques, not bonding with others, and that's where a good management structure comes in.

In 1977, there was a good bit of controversy about the 'three-stripe affair'. The County Board were suspending Jimmy Barr and Brian Murphy because they wore the stripes down in Killarney, but we said that they were part of our team and that if they were going, we were all going.

We were down training one night and the chairman Donal O'Sullivan came into the dressing-room. 'Right lads!' he said. 'Hands up who's wearing that three-stripe gear?' We said we were all wearing it and Donal said that we'd have to pull out of the championship. The response was that that was no problem, we'd go with the two lads.

We went down to the Beamish Rooms to discuss it – and have a few pints! – and we came back up to the dressing-room and the board said they'd reinstate the lads, but we'd have to wear the official gear.

We kept the adidas stuff for training. After that, we beat Galway, so we were into another final against Wexford. The feeling was that a good team could win one All-Ireland but it took a great team to win two... but that also brought its own pressure.

We stayed in the Central Hotel. Myself and Mick Malone were always great friends and we used to share a room. The two of us and Seánie O'Leary used to go out and the boys would have two pints and I've have a rock shandy. We'd come back and have a cup of tea then before bed.

The morning of a final, I wouldn't get up until around 11 o'clock. I'd sleep for seven or eight hours but then I'd meditate for another two hours on my own – I looked at it as wanting to get all the mistakes that I might make out of my head! It's a natural tendency to underestimate yourself so I wanted to build myself up for the good things that I should do.

You don't want to get carried away, either – as the man says, you'd want to get your head level. The match was 70 minutes but, really, it takes three weeks to play an All-Ireland.

After Wexford's two goals, we were hanging on but I managed to bring off saves from Christy Keogh, and then John Quigley, and we held out. To go back-to-back was special and it was part of Cork hurling history.

Ringy was the maestro and we did it for him, too.

I remember at one stage I cleared a ball and there was a huge cheer. I thought I must be the most popular goalkeeper in Ireland, but I turned around and there was Ring, behind the goal – they were shouting for him and not for me!

He was special. It's like all great men, he had to die to be really appreciated.

TOM CASHMAN

CORK 0-13 CLARE 0-11
Munster SHC Final
Semple Stadium
JULY 30, 1978

Cork captain Tom Cashman lifts the Liam MacCarthy Cup after victory over Galway in 1986, but eight years earlier he had the greatest experience of his county career when defeating Clare in the Munster final.

★ **CORK:** M Coleman; D Burns, M O'Doherty, J Horgan (0-4); D McCurtain, J Crowley, D Coughlan; **T Cashman (0-1)**, T Crowley (0-1); G McCarthy, J Barry-Murphy, P Moylan; C McCarthy (0-5), R Cummins (0-2), M Malone. Subs: E O'Donoghue for Malone, P Horgan for Moylan.

★ **CLARE:** S Durack; J O'Gorman, J Power, J McMahon; G Loughnane (0-1), S Hehir, S Stack; M Moroney (0-1), J Callinan (0-1); J McNamara, N Casey (0-1), C Honan (0-6); P O'Connor, M McKeogh, E O'Connor (0-1). Subs: B Gilligan for McKeogh.

THE ACTION

NOT SINCE LIMERICK from 1934-37 had a Munster hurling four in-a-row been achieved – while Cork won four All-Irelands on the trot from 1941-44, they had lost the 1941 Munster decider, played after the All-Ireland, to a Tipperary side that had been unable to field earlier in the year due to an outbreak of Foot and Mouth disease.

As with 1977, Cork faced Clare, who were National League champions for the second year in-a-row and who had Justin McCarthy as coach to manager Fr Harry Bohan. When Cork, afflicted by poor shooting and missing Brian Murphy and Seánie O'Leary, could only assemble a first-half lead of 0-5 to 0-3 after playing with the wind, it seemed as if it would be the Banner's day to end a wait dating back to 1932.

Instead, Cork showed the grit and resolve that had won them the previous two All-Ireland titles and now left them just one game away from doing the three in-a-row. In his report, *The Cork Examiner's* Jim O'Sullivan noted a key factor in the narrow victory... *Tom Cashman's display of pure hurling skill – so vital in launching Cork to victory – was the highlight and it made him my man of the match for the second successive year.*

Cork had four wides before a long-range free went over from corner-back John Horgan. Though Martin Coleman's puckouts were dropping about 40 yards from the Clare goal, their backs were well on top against an under-performing Cork attacking unit.

However, on the resumption, it was clear that the Clare forwards were suffering from the same malaise as their Cork counterparts had in the first period, and the Cork defence excelled in such circumstances. Denis Burns – in for Murphy – Martin O'Doherty and Dermot McCurtain were stout and resilient while Coleman's puckouts gave relief as, even against the wind, they reached midfield.

With Cashman continuing to dominate at midfield – now partnered by Pat Moylan – Cork made progress and Charlie McCarthy was able to convert the frees that accrued. With 12 minutes to go, Cork were five points clear – 0-12 to 0-7 – and, though this advantage was eroded after Clare points from Colm Honan (two) and John Callinan, Charlie McCarthy's fifth pointed free of the day gave some breathing space again before Ger Loughnane finished off the scoring.

★★★★★

66

THE GAME THAT stands out to me down through the years would be the 1978 Munster final.

Cork were going for a fourth Munster in-a-row and had won the last two All-Irelands. As well as that, there was a sub-plot in the fact that we were playing Clare again. The 1977 season was part and parcel of '78 because Clare had won two National Leagues and Justin McCarthy was involved with them.

In the Munster Championship match against them in 1977 there was hassle between Jim Power and Ray Cummins and, whatever happened, Power was sent off. Clare were flying, they had a great team, and it was a huge disappointment for them to lose in '77 – I think they were expecting to win that match.

They felt that Power shouldn't have been sent off and that left a sour taste for them. If it happened now, it'd be shown on slow-motion 50 times, but it happened so fast that it was missed by nearly everyone!

Minor was the first time you got to play for Cork. Blackrock and St Michael's won the county double in 1974 and I was lucky enough to be on the two Cork teams that won the All-Ireland double. I was minor again in 1975, but Kilkenny beat us in the All-Ireland hurling final and Kerry beat us in Munster in the football.

Dermot McCurtain and myself came on to the panel after the first round of the league in 1976, when we were 19, just out of minor. The two of us and Tim Crowley established ourselves on the team then and stayed until the mid-80s. It was great to come on to a panel that had just won the All-Ireland and be able to play alongside the likes of Ray Cummins, Denis Coughlan, Gerald McCarthy and Charlie McCarthy.

At the same time, it didn't feel like a huge step up to be playing senior for Cork. Myself and Dermot came on to the Blackrock senior team when we were minor and they would have had six or seven players on the Cork team at the time, as well as Frank Cummins playing for Kilkenny.

The fact that the county senior championship was so strong at the time meant that the leap to senior inter-county wasn't overly dramatic. For Blackrock, I was playing alongside the likes of Ray and Frank Cummins, John Horgan, Pat Moylan, Eamonn O'Donoghue, and we were coming up against the Glen and the Barrs, who had a lot of inter-county players too. Going into the Cork dressing-room, it was great to be playing alongside those players rather than playing against them, and all of the more experienced players made me and the rest of the newcomers feel welcome. It was a great experience.

When we came into the team, we were accepted straightaway and we were told that we'd learn our apprenticeship with those guys… and we did. Hoggy was tremendous that day. In your first couple of years, to start off and win two All-Irelands was fantastic. The hope then was that the experience you'd gain from these guys could be passed on to the lads coming on in the 1980s. It was a great learning curve.

Coaching wasn't as big a thing back then and it was mostly left to the players to work on things themselves. When you had Seánie O'Leary, Ray and Charlie in the full-forward line, it was about getting the ball into them as quickly as you could! I would have been familiar with Fr Michael O'Brien from the minor teams, and then with Blackrock as well, and then at senior level for Cork there was another priest in charge – Fr Bertie Troy. He had a great record at minor and under-21 and would then go on to manage the teams for the three in-a-row, so you have to give him credit.

As well as that, there were some players with great experience – Denis Coughlan and Gerald would have been like father figures. Kevin Kehilly was the physical trainer at the time and the team was super-fit.

We wouldn't have played against Clare much – maybe at under-21, but we didn't know what to expect. When you look at the players they had, with Séamus Durack in goal and the half-back line of Ger Loughnane, Seán Stack and Seán Hehir, they were a serious team. They'd Johnny Callinan and Mick Moroney, Colm Honan, Jackie O'Gorman… they had a fantastic team. The two National Leagues that they'd won, they won convincingly, beating Kilkenny in the final both years.

On the Saturday before a game, myself and Dermot used to go over to Blackrock at around 12 o'clock, have a small warm-up and a puck-around. That was the only thing I had in terms of a ritual, though in 1977 there had been a break from that. I was involved with a youth club and they were going up to

Donegal just before the All-Ireland final. I got permission to go, so I came from Donegal with the club on the Saturday and joined the team at the hotel. We beat Wexford, so my preparations must have helped!

Back then, when Cork won the toss, they used to play against the wind, but that day in 1978 we lost the toss and Clare decided to play against it. It was a full house in Thurles and it was a dog-fight, in a gale of wind. They were down after 1977, so we were expecting a real backlash.

I was in midfield with Tim Crowley. Gerald would have been midfield with Pat Moylan the previous year, and then Timmy and myself came in. About two years later, when John Fenton came in and made midfield his own, Gerald and Timmy and myself were in the half-forward line! Once you could hurl, you could play anywhere, really.

I remember at the start of the game, Moroney and Callinan were fighting – one was to pick up me and the other Timmy, but our instructions were to do the opposite. It meant that for the first five minutes, there were four of us together! We won the first few balls so they had to do something and Moroney came on me and Callinan on Timmy, so that worked in our favour a bit.

Even with the wind, we were only ahead by 0-5 to 0-3 at half-time and I think Hoggy got four of those from '65s' or frees. It was that kind of a game but, coming in, I've never heard such a roar as I did that day from the Clare supporters. They clapped and roared the team off at half-time and the noise was as if they had won the match. They were obviously doing it to spur on Clare, but it had a galvanising effect on us. I remember at half-time, Christy Ring spoke inside in the dressing-room and it really got us going.

The three in-a-row was never really spoken about at all at the time. With the experienced players that were there, they were all cool characters and professionals in their own way. There was no going on drinking sessions or anything, the team was totally honest and gave one hundred percent and were willing to back each other up.

John Horgan in the full-back line, Martin O'Doherty, Johnny Crowley centre-back – he was only a year older than us but he never looked inexperienced – and then Charlie, Ray and Seánie inside in the full-forward line. For God's sake, if you didn't get the ball in fast to them, they wouldn't be long letting you know!

At half-time, our instructions were to keep it a low-scoring game, keep it boring. The backs were fantastic. The second-half was backs-to-the-wall again... defend, defend... DEFEND. The final score was 0-13 to 0-11 and I think Charlie got five for us, mainly from frees, and Hoggy got his four. Colm Honan did most of the scoring for them. It was a dog-fight of a match and it was a great game to win, under the circumstances.

That Clare team never went on to win a Munster. I remember talking to Séamus Durack later and he said that the only time he played in Croke Park was in the Railway Cup for Munster! They were unlucky because they were a great team and they certainly would have deserved more than two National Leagues. They wanted to win Munster... the county hadn't won one since the 1920s and there was talk about the curse of Biddy Early, which lasted until they won the All-Ireland in 1995.

I played with a few of them for Munster and they were all fantastic characters and really good players, but they were just unlucky, really.

You can win nice or you can win ugly, and we won ugly that day.

It was a game that would stand out in terms of the team being able to come out with the result when our backs were to the wall. It was the middle of a Munster five in-a-row and even though we lost in Munster in 1980 and '81, we won the National League both years.

That team was used to winning... there was a great bunch of guys there.

GER CUNNINGHAM

CORK 4-15 TIPPERARY 3-14
Munster SHC Final
Semple Stadium
JULY 15, 1984

Inspired by the hooped jersey worn by Billy Morgan in the 1973 All-Ireland final, Ger Cunningham (above, in the mid-90s) also chose a hooped shirt throughout his career, including his most memorable game, the 1984 Munster final victory over Tipperary.

★ **CORK: G Cunningham**; D Mulcahy, D O'Grady, J Hodgins; T Cashman, J Crowley, D McCurtain; J Fenton (0-7), P Hartnett (0-1); P Horgan (0-3), T Crowley, K Hennessy (0-3); T Mulcahy, J Barry-Murphy (2-0), S O'Leary (1-1). Subs: J Blake for O'Grady, T O'Sullivan (1-0) for T Crowley, D Walsh for Horgan.

★ **TIPPERARY:** J Sheedy; J Bergin, J Keogh, D Cahill; P Fitzelle, J McIntyre, B Ryan; R Callaghan, P Kennedy (0-2); N English (1-0), D O'Connell (1-2), L Maher (0-1); M Doyle, S Power (1-6), N O'Dwyer (0-2). Subs: J Doyle for Cahill, B Heffernan for Fitzelle, P Dooley (0-1) for Ryan.

THE ACTION

1984 BROUGHT EXTRA motivation for every county, as the GAA celebrated its 100th birthday and Cork, now under the management of Justin McCarthy and Fr Michael O'Brien, won the open draw format competition, the Centenary Cup, beating Laois in the final in Croke Park, before overcoming Limerick in the Munster semi-final at the Gaelic Grounds.

That set up an 'old firm' Munster final against a resurgent Tipperary – the first since 1970. In 1984, Tipp had an additional carrot in the fact that the All-Ireland final would be held in Semple Stadium, and so, things were at fever pitch on Munster final day.

After Kevin Hennessy's opening point for Cork, Tipp had a massive boost as Séamus Power scored a goal. However, Cork looked to have settled as Jimmy Barry-Murphy netted twice in quick succession, in the 11th and 15th minutes, but as half-time approached Tipp stayed in it as Donie O'Connell and then English both raised green flags. It left Cork ahead by 2-10 to 3-5 at the break.

Power cut the lead early in the second-half but, while Hennessy replied for Cork on 40, they were to score just once more in the 25 scoreless minutes thereafter. In between, Tipp looked for all the world as if they would end their famine.

Centre-back John McIntyre was majestic for the home side, who levelled as sub Paul Dooley pointed with his first touch, before Liam Maher put them in front. Though the excellent Pat Hartnett tied the game again, Power tapped a penalty over before Noel O'Dwyer gave Tipp a two-point lead. It was doubled through a Philip Kennedy '70' and an O'Dwyer free – Tipp four ahead with seven minutes left, 3-14 to 2-13.

Cork did not waver and they were rewarded as John Fenton's free was followed by a levelling goal from sub Tony O'Sullivan in the wake of a John Sheedy save from Hartnett. More drama was to follow, though not before a vital Denis Mulcahy intervention to prevent what would have been a certain Tipp goal. The ball was worked to O'Sullivan, who went for a point. Goalkeeper Sheedy tried to stop the ball going over the bar and did so but, unfortunately for him, Seánie O'Leary was lurking and fired home from close range. Fenton clinched it as Cork won by four.

★★★★★

"

MY CHOICE IS unusual perhaps because, while it was a fantastic game and a great occasion, it's not one I'd look back on with huge fondness with regard to my own performance.

I had grown up going to Cork-Tipperary Munster finals. At the time, I was working for Dwans of Thurles – our depot was in Fermoy, and I was based in Cork. There were some fanatical hurling people involved. Pat Stakelum, a Tipp selector at the time, was a colleague of mine, as was Seán McLoughlin, who used to play for Tipp. Pat had captained Tipp to win the 1949 All-Ireland and had three medals, while Seán had four – I had lost in 1982 and '83, so you can imagine the slagging and pressure that came with that!

It was massive to have us involved, but I completely over-trained the week of that match. There was so much happening and so much going on, I left it all on the training pitch. I did extra training that I shouldn't have done – I didn't trust what I had under my belt and I wanted to be so ready for it that I over-analysed it.

I wasn't sharp on the day. That said, the All-Ireland final against Offaly that year was the opposite, as I had learned from my mistakes in the Munster final. I made sure never to overcook myself again.

My first game for Cork seniors was a challenge match in May 1980 – I had just returned from a soccer trial with Celtic, having won the All-Ireland Cup that year with my local side Tramore Athletic. Back then, you'd often have games on Sunday nights for opening pitches – Cork were going up to Carrickshock to play Kilkenny and I got a call at home at lunchtime on the Sunday to know if I'd travel.

I was still only 18, but I had played for the Barrs in 1979 and we reached the county final. We were beaten by Blackrock. That was a great learning curve. I made the championship panel for 1980… Timmy Murphy was in goal.

In October 1980, I was picked to play in the league and kept the spot for the championship but it was a straight knockout back then and we were beaten by Clare in '81. That was a short enough championship year… I think we lost Ray Cummins beforehand. Obviously, I had no clue that I'd play every championship game for the next 17 years – you just don't know at that stage, you're living from game to game and year to year.

I had been Cork minor hurling goalkeeper in 1978 and '79, and we won the All-Ireland both years. That was my first time coming across the Canon. He had been there in 1977 and I got a trial that year when I was under-16, just after I had started playing in goal. I used to play out the field before that – the change happened in school, Coláiste Eamann Rís in Deerpark. Pat McDonnell, who played full-back for Cork, was one of the coaches there at the time and Andy Creagh from Blackrock was another one. Billy Morgan was in the school, too.

Tony Mullins played in goal at the time… he was an excellent keeper, and, whatever the reasons were, they ended up swapping us. Then the Barrs did the same and we won the under-16 county in 1977. I had no issue at all. Once I got in there, I enjoyed it and it went from there. I wasn't good enough to make it out the field!

I was the Cork minor football goalkeeper in 1979 too, but it wasn't a difficult choice to plump for hurling, really, as it was always my first love. What made it easier was that another St Finbarr's goalkeeper, John Kerins, God be good to him, was behind me and he was the dual Cork minor keeper in 1980. As we went up the ages, we ended up subbing for each other – he played in goal in football, and I did in the hurling. I knew hurling was the one for me and Kerinsy was better at football so there was no issue, it fell nicely that way.

Back then, there was no goalkeeping coaching, only stuff that you'd do on your own. You'd pick up bits and pieces from different people and I would have been a big believer in going to the ball alley. I was lucky that I had gone to Deerpark at a time when Billy Morgan was there and, when I started playing in goal, we used to do a lot of training together, specific goalkeeping stuff.

That was the first time I came across anything like that. We used to do football and hurling stuff. In terms of long puck-outs, I always had a good belt of a ball and whether it was a factor in me being put in goal, I don't know. After I moved, I certainly spent quite a bit of time practising it.

The fact that the Barrs were successful – we got to six county finals in-a-row – was a big help in terms of making the step up to senior inter-county. It meant you were playing at a good level all the time, which was good. Midleton came at that time as well and really made a big impact. They became our arch-rivals, really. They were very strong… they had a great team. We played them in 1979; it was a special game, a semi-final down in Riverstown. They had won the intermediate the year before and that was the first time they put their hand up. We beat them in four straight semi-finals, before they beat us in 1983.

Obviously, Cork lost the All-Ireland finals to Kilkenny in 1982 and '83. We had come through so easily in '82 – we won the Munster final handily enough against Waterford and we went in as favourites. It was a bit of a shock to us really that we lost to Kilkenny; it was my first time losing to them. You're obviously looking to win your first All-Ireland medal and that was a missed opportunity, obviously. Looking back on the 1983 final, I think it was a game that we should have won. It was a horrific day, very windy, and we missed six or seven frees if memory serves me right. That was very disappointing… to lose two in-a-row was tough.

Johnny Clifford was in charge in 1983 but he wasn't elected when the County Board were picking the selectors for '84. Five selectors were voted in – Justin, the Canon, Tom Monaghan, Denis Hurley and Joe Desmond – and there was no manager appointed. Justin and the Canon became joint coaches.

They were rivals on the coaching front at the time, so it was definitely a surprise that the two of them were appointed that way – they were usually on the opposite sides… and now they were going to have to work together.

They were two completely different characters, and poles apart in their approach. There was still a very good team there; we had got to the previous two All-Irelands, so you were still going to be very competitive.

Normally you'd have one guy calling the shots, but we had two very strong characters. Donie Wallace, the former Cork Hibernians great, helped out on the strength and conditioning side and did some goalkeeper training.

We won the Centenary Cup… we beat Laois in the final. We had beaten Roscommon, Clare and Offaly to get to it, and Laois beat Galway in their semi-final so it was a novel pairing. That fact that we had won a national competition in Croke Park definitely helped, given that we had lost the last two All-Ireland finals. It set us up, it was a good springboard. We beat Limerick in Limerick to reach the Munster final against Tipp. They hadn't been competitive in a while and had been off the scene a few years.

I always made sure to go to the alley the week of a game, usually with Justin. It was a good way of honing my skills and keeping my eye in – though I nearly took my eye out there in 1985! Some nights you might go to training and end up doing very little, compared to now where the keeper would have his own drills and exercises, and work on particular things. You'd play a game and find that you mightn't get too much work done on the night, depending on what was being focused on.

I always liked to get my main hurley reshaped or touched up coming up to a big game. Fellas now would have four or five different hurleys, as they're more likely to break due to the bigger base, but back then you'd have a favourite one and want to have it right for the day. I'd always re-grip it too.

Justin was very much into repairing hurleys. He was brilliant at touching them up and fixing them, getting the weight, size and shape right for the particular game. It was great to have someone like that involved and my cousin Cormac Finn was very good at it too. Sonny McCarthy from Killeagh and Mick McCarthy from Glanmire also made great hurleys for me.

I didn't wear a helmet at the time but, after I got concussed against Waterford in 1989, I wore one for a while that didn't have a facemask. When we won the All-Ireland in 1990, I wore a black and blue Cooper.

That win in 1990 was my seventh All-Ireland medal with Cork – three senior, two under-21 and two minor – and in each final I wore a red-and-white hooped jersey. I think the grá for the hoops came from Billy in 1973. Cork wore white against Galway and so he had to switch to the hooped top. Because he was in the school, it had a strong impact on me.

It made me feel better than wearing a plain white one. Even with the Barrs later on, I used to wear hoops, either blue and white or blue and yellow.

We used to go to the matches by car… there'd be cars going from different parts of Cork. Tom Buttimer from Ballinhassig was my driver… he'd collect me at home and then we'd meet inside in St Patrick's Quay and then go off in a convoy up to Thurles. There was a great relationship between the players and drivers, as you travelled with the same fellas all the time. You'd be fairly relaxed, mixed with a bit of excitement.

Going to Thurles was always enjoyable, especially when there was a full house, as there was a good atmosphere, but that day was very special, with the Tipp factor added in. They'd have fancied their chances playing in Thurles.

Those chances increased when they got a goal with nearly their first play. A ball in over the full-back line, a long clearance... and just as I went to play it, Séamus Power got his hurley to it. It was probably poor play from me and brilliant play from him, but it wasn't the ideal start you wanted in a Munster final. A big day... and your first thing to do is pick the ball out of the net.

A modern-day sports psychologist would be encouraging you to have your little triggers to move on when you make a mistake – refocus and reset – but back then you were just waiting for the next ball. I knew at that stage I was flat enough and it was one of those games where you were nearly hoping that the ball wouldn't come, as you were afraid of making a mistake.

They stayed in it and they were four points ahead nearing the end, but their selectors had made a crazy decision when Bobby Ryan got injured – they moved Power, who was having a great game at full-forward, to corner-back. Even still, it looked like Tipp's day. You're just praying at that stage.

I can remember the Michael Doyle chance as if it was yesterday. He had a chance to put the ball over the bar, and five points at that stage might have been too much to come back from, but he tried to handpass across to Nicky English and Denis Mulcahy intercepted it... and cleared down the field to Tony O'Sullivan. Tony went for the point and that led to Seánie's goal, which was the turning point.

The scenes at the end were phenomenal. We had come from four points down to win by four, which was huge, though that can happen in hurling. For me, relief was the over-riding emotion. You knew yourself that we had got away with one and we were into the All-Ireland semi-final against Antrim, so we had a good chance of making it back to the final.

To have been part of Tony O'Sullivan's only goal for Cork was also special! We used to be slagging him – he scored two thousand points, and one goal. To be fair, he also got one against Tipperary down in Killarney in 1987 but that was disallowed.

Going on to beat Offaly in Thurles was the perfect end to the year.

It was special because it was my first medal and because I was working for a Thurles company. Dwans made a presentation to me after the All-Ireland final before we got on the bus... that made it extra-special as we had beaten Tipp along the way.

99

JOHN FENTON
(& JOHNNY CROWLEY)

CORK 3-16   OFFALY 1-12
All-Ireland SHC Final
Semple Stadium
SEPTEMBER 2, 1984

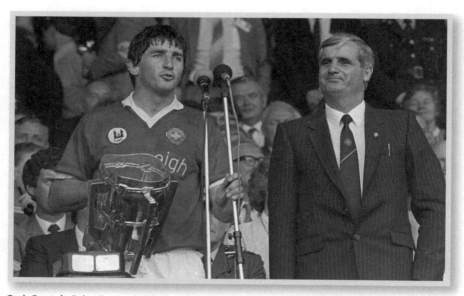

Cork Captain John Fenton holds the Liam MacCarthy Cup after being presented with the trophy by GAA President Paddy Buggy at the end of the Centenary All-Ireland final in 1984.

★ **CORK:** G Cunningham; D Mulcahy, D O'Grady, J Hodgins; T Cashman, **J Crowley**, D McCurtain; **J Fenton (0-7)**, P Hartnett (0-1); K Hennessy (1-0), T Crowley, T O'Sullivan (0-6); T Mulcahy (0-1), J Barry-Murphy, S O'Leary (2-1).

★ **OFFALY:** D Martin; L Carroll, E Coughlan, P Fleury; A Fogarty, P Delaney (0-4), G Coughlan; T Connelly, J Kelly; M Corrigan (1-2), B Bermingham, P Carroll (0-4); D Fogarty, P Horan (0-2), J Dooley. Subs: P Corrigan for Bermingham, P Kirwan for Dooley.

THE ACTION

AFTER BEATING TIPPERARY in the Munster final, Cork saw off Antrim in the All-Ireland semi-final in Croke Park, before returning to Thurles for the Centenary All-Ireland final – the last time the showpiece game had been held outside of Croke Park was when Tipperary beat Kilkenny in Killarney in 1937. Offaly were Cork's opponents – the first time the counties clashed in the senior championship.

The Faithful County had claimed their maiden title in 1981 – as of 2022, they are the most recent first-time champions – and Cork were seeking to avoid losing three finals in-a-row, which would have been a first. Prior to the game, all living All-Ireland final captains were presented to the crowd. The roll-call began with Kilkenny's 1983 captain Liam Fennelly and ended with 84-year-old Eudie Coughlan of Cork, who had led the Rebels past Kilkenny after a three-game saga in 1931. That would prove a positive omen, albeit without the need for any replays.

The game took time to settle, with each side unable to capitalise on half-chances for goals, though Johnny Crowley at centre-back and the midfield pairing of captain John Fenton and Pat Hartnett helped to give Cork a platform. The sides had been level four times before Mark Corrigan and Pat Carroll put Offaly in to a two-point lead, but Seánie O'Leary's goal nine minutes before half-time ensured that Cork led at the break by 1-5 to 0-7.

The opening 14 minutes of the second-half brought six unanswered points for Cork – Fenton with three, Tony O'Sullivan scoring two and O'Leary also on target – before the second goal. Kevin Hennessy won possession and laid off to Jimmy Barry-Murphy whose shot was saved by Damien Martin, but left in the path of Hennessy, who had an easy finish.

A 2-11 to 0-7 lead was unlikely to be overhauled, especially as a Joe Dooley goal attempt for Offaly was repelled by Ger Cunningham just after that. While a Pat Delaney '65' finally ended Offaly's scoring drought, Cork replied with their third goal, O'Leary's second, as he got on the end of a Johnny Crowley clearance.

Ten points separated the sides at the end, with Cork able to enjoy the closing stages after the disappointment of the previous two finals.

★★★★★

66

FROM A PERSONAL point of view, the 1984 All-Ireland final capped a wonderful year for me.

I first played with Cork in 1975, coming on as a sub in the Munster Championship when I was 20. I was in and out of the team then for a few years after that... I played championship in 1976, I wasn't really there in '77. I was a sub on the All-Ireland final team in 1978, but from then on, I was involved on a regular basis.

In 1978, I captained Midleton to win the county Intermediate Championship and we reached the next four senior semi-finals against St Finbarr's, and lost them all before making the big breakthrough in 1983, when we won the senior title.

I would take the year from the All-Ireland final of 1983 to the one in '84 as encapsulating the highs and the lows. The 1983 All-Ireland was a low point for me, both personally and in terms of the team. I was taken off, and I came very close to not playing again afterwards. Only for Dr Con Murphy and Johnny Clifford having a few words with me in the dressing-room after the game, I would probably have quit the county scene.

A month after the All-Ireland final, Midleton were in the county final against the Barrs and we won it, the club's first senior title since 1916. After winning the county title we defeated Borrisoleigh in the Munster club final, and I was lucky enough to captain the team to these victories. Winning the county senior title meant that Midleton could nominate the Cork captain for the following year... and I was nominated for that role in 1984.

Cork won the Centenary Cup... and I captained Munster to win the Railway Cup, and obviously there was the Munster Championship and the All-Ireland. The only trophy that was missing was the National League that was won by Limerick, who defeated Wexford in the final after they got the better of us in the semi-final.

Winning the county championship probably gave us extra confidence. It was no fluke that... if you looked at the Midleton and Barrs teams that played in the county final in 1983, they constituted over half the panel involved with Cork in '84. You contrast that with now, when you'd be lucky to have one or two county players involved in the county final.

In 1984, we had seven players on the panel that won the Centenary Cup and six for the championship season, with four – Denis Mulcahy, Pat Hartnett, Kevin Hennessy and myself – starting, and Ger Power and John Hartnett also on the panel. Joe Desmond from Midleton was also chairman of the selection committee.

The club rivalry was never a problem when we got together to play for Cork. One thing I always said was that, when you went into a Cork dressing-room, from the first day to the last, you were a Cork player, irrespective of what club you were from or whatever happened on the field in club matches. We had a fairly tempestuous game with the Barrs in the county championship in 1984 and they beat us, but the next week we were back in training and the club game was never even mentioned. On that night, we were all Cork players and there was never any conflict of interest.

Justin McCarthy and Fr Michael O'Brien were the new joint-coaches, and there was a change of emphasis... it freshened things up. We went into 1984 on the back of two bad All-Ireland final defeats – we had won the Munster Championship fairly easily on both occasions, but Kilkenny had beaten us well in 1982, though there wasn't so much of a difference in '83.

It was a case of two new voices. Justin and the Canon were both very powerful and strong in their opinions, and they were both singing from the one hymn sheet. It meant two big Cork voices behind us, and it gave the team added impetus and self-belief.

Scores from dead balls weren't as big a factor as they are now, but they were still important. I used to train a lot on my own when I was a young lad. I was exceedingly lucky that the gable end wall of my house was my first hurling 'ground'. Then, we had an old golf course next to where I lived, and I spent a lot of time out there, practicing frees and sideline pucks. I would regularly go to the CBS pitch or our own pitch, taking frees on my own.

When we'd go training with Cork, Ger Cunningham and myself would often go in early or stay late – I'd practice frees and he'd practice hitting puckouts. We helped each other that way... I'd also done this with Ger Power, our Midleton goalkeeper.

Cork beat Limerick in the Munster semi-final and that set up a first final against Tipperary since 1970. Tipp were hell-bent on trying to win that game, as the All-Ireland final was going to be in Thurles to mark the centenary and there was a fierce tension around the ground that day.

A lot of the time, in games like that, you're aware of the crowd but it's background noise. When Tipperary went four points up with four or five minutes to go, the shout that went out from their supporters was deafening – you often hear the expression that the roof came off the stand, but I honestly thought it would be lifted off! It was a wake-up call for us, really… we knew it was down to the wire.

To be able to come back and win by four points was testament to the hurling and the character of the players on the Cork team and the set-up at the time.

We then had Antrim in the All-Ireland semi-final in Croke Park. We approached that game with all seriousness as we were aware of their pride and skill. This was an Antrim team on the way up and they proved this a few years later when they would go on to shock Offaly in an All-Ireland semi-final. They had some fabulous players at the time, but we were determined to get back to another All-Ireland final having lost the previous two. We knew what we had to do, we didn't take any chances and we clicked on the day.

That meant it was back to Thurles for the All-Ireland final and, I suppose, it was an advantage in the same way that playing in Croke Park is for Leinster teams.

If it had been Kilkenny there, they might have been used to playing in Thurles more often, but Offaly were an emerging team and probably didn't have as much experience of it and Croke Park would have suited them at the time – not that that would have fazed us either.

We didn't want to be the first Cork team to lose three All-Ireland finals in-a-row. It didn't put any extra pressure on us as such, but it was in the background. I can't recall if it was ever spoken about coming up to the game… I doubt if it was, but you'd have seen it in the press or whatever. *Was it a factor?* Probably not.

I had captained a lot of teams coming up along the line; it was something I was fairly used to and this was a very easy group to lead. You had leaders on the pitch, leaders on the coaching side, leaders on the selectorial side. I didn't feel any extra pressure because I was the captain. I knew that I just had to perform to the best of my ability and that the rest of the players would do the same.

Under normal circumstances, we would have travelled to Thurles by car… four or five players to a car. On that occasion, they didn't want to take any chances with traffic or cars breaking down – not that that ever happened! – so, we were told to be at Kent Station on the Sunday morning. We got the train to Thurles, which was most unusual, and we didn't know where we were going when we got there... nor were we told.

After we reached Thurles, we got on a bus – just the panel and the selectors – and we had two garda outriders, who took us to the gates of the Ursuline Convent. We drove in, the gates were closed behind us and we spent the next few hours with the nuns in their convent grounds... and it was absolutely fabulous.

Fr O'Brien was the chaplain to the Cistercian Order in Blackrock and he arranged it through them. We had a puck-around – we had to show the nuns how to hurl, too! – and we went in then and had Mass... and it was powerful. The last hymn coming out was *Faith of Our Fathers* and every fella belted it out.

Up then for the tea and sandwiches... and it was all red and white napkins. We'd no interference, no interaction with anybody else... only ourselves.

Derry Gowen was the chairman of the County Board at the time and, of course, he knew where we had gone. He turned up at the convent gates. He told them who he was, but he was told that there was no Cork team there... and he wasn't allowed in, so he had to go away! The two garda outriders had stayed with us and, while we were upstairs having the team meeting, the nuns were outside with the gardaí, sitting on the motor bikes and getting spins out to the gates and back!

From what I can remember, Offaly were in two different hotels on that day, so that didn't help their preparation. Such was our preparation before the game, that we promised the nuns before we left that – win, lose or draw – we'd be back the following day. On the Monday morning, two bus-loads left the hotel at 11am for the convent and there was nobody late. The excitement and reception we received from the nuns when we arrived back with the trophy will stay with us for all our days.

We wore special once-off jerseys for the centenary final, with 'Corcaigh' across the front and the GAA centenary logo and Cork crest. I don't know whose decision it was – I presume it was the executive of the County Board or the management. We were shown the jerseys on the Wednesday night at training and had a team photograph taken, then we were given them again in the dressing-room in Thurles on the day of the game.

Pat Hartnett, my Midleton clubmate, was my midfield partner. He would normally play wing-back for Midleton but that Cork team had been together for a while, so playing in that team was playing in a club team, as such. We all knew each other's style and how we would hurl. It was a different game to now in that there was more room around the centre of the field. The ball was heavier, it wouldn't travel as fast and a very good puckout from a goalkeeper would land as far as the opposing half-back line… that's as far as it would go. There was a lot of interaction then when the ball was broken down and you were always involved in the game.

Somebody once described centrefield play as being like a postman – you collect the ball and you deliver it. That's the way we were taught, and we had a forward line with the likes of Jimmy Barry-Murphy, Kevin Hennessy, Ray Cummins, Seánie O'Leary, Charlie McCarthy, Tony O'Sullivan, Tomás Mulcahy… all that these lads wanted was good, quick, fast ball from midfield. They didn't want it put into their hands, necessarily, but once it came in hard and fast, they were happy and it's the way we trained – get the ball into the full-forward line.

We had the most lethal forward line in the country and, the more ball you gave them, the more chances they had of scoring. You could see that in the All-Ireland final – Seánie got two goals, and Kevin Hennessy got the third.

It was 1-5 to 0-7 at half-time, so it was there or thereabouts, but in the second-half we scored 2-11 while restricting Offaly to 1-5. The longer the game went on, the more we were going to win by. From that point of view, as a spectacle it was probably a bit of an anti-climax coming up to the end but, from a Cork point of view, that didn't really bother us. All that we were interested in was the win.

We were sure enough in the last five minutes that, barring something catastrophic happening, we were probably going to win. I won't say we took our foot off the pedal, that didn't happen, but the pressure that had been there in the Tipperary game wasn't there for the Offaly game in the last five minutes.

There was a fantastic atmosphere as usual around Thurles, and a great crowd in Cork the following night when we got to Saint Patrick's Street. On the Tuesday we went to Beamish, which was a tradition at the time after an All-Ireland final, with the great entertainer and Cork supporter Billa O'Connell, a Beamish employee, providing the craic and banter. We had a great day there and it was down to Midleton that night for a parade. There was a brilliant buzz around the area and a huge crowd in Midleton that night, with the team being led up the town by the Midleton Brass and Reed Band... led by my uncle Dick Cashman. After that, it was localised in the sense that we went around to different clubs and schools with the cup as is the norm.

That was the big difference I noticed from being a winning captain... the number of functions that had to be attended. The months after the All-Ireland final, in terms of commitment and time, were worse than the three months before the final!

But you'd put up with that, after captaining that great Cork team to the Centenary All-Ireland Championship.

JOHNNY CROWLEY

Johnny Crowley has words with the referee during Cork's victory over Tipperary in the Munster final in 1984.

"

IT WAS THE centenary final, and we had lost the two prior to it in 1982 and '83.

I had been on the three in-a-row team, and then in 1979 we lost to Galway in the All-Ireland semi-final… and Limerick beat us in '80, and Clare knocked us out in '81. The losses to Kilkenny in 1982 and '83 were very disappointing.

We had chances in both, but we didn't take them and that's sport. Kilkenny were good too, to be fair, and there wasn't much in the games. Sometimes matches just go away from you and, against Kilkenny, it's very hard to drag it back.

After that, there were a lot of people questioning us and a few fellas retired as well, so the pressure was on. The media were wondering if it was the end for that team — nothing changes really, does it?! We knew we were capable enough, that we had good players and that we hadn't been far off it in the previous two years.

We had still won Munster and got to the two finals, so it was a case of sticking with it.

There was such hype attached to 1984 because of the year that it was, and then playing in Thurles was like a home game for us because we were used to it. I could have picked the first All-Ireland or the last one in 1986, but '84 just stands out in my head.

I'm originally from Enniskeane in West Cork. I was born in 1956 and we moved to Bishopstown in '63 – I came in under the Viaduct! My father was an agricultural advisor and he was transferred in to Cork. He worked from home and used to call to farmers – he was over grants and things like that.

Nowadays, Bishopstown is a suburb of the city but back then it was in the countryside, too. Where Cork University Hospital, or the Regional as it was originally known, is now, that was where we played soccer and fellas would go on their bikes... 'the Mounds' as we called it. The club had only been founded in 1956 and my father became involved in it when we came in. Bishopstown won the county Intermediate Football Championship in 1974 and I was a dual Cork minor the same year – we won the All-Ireland double.

I had gone to Coláiste an Spioraid Naoimh in Bishopstown up to the Inter Cert. I have three brothers and they all went to Farranferris – there was a strong tradition of West Cork fellas boarding there – so there was kind of an expectation that I would go there sometime, so I went up there after the Inter. Fr O'Brien was there and my brother Michael had won a Harty in 1972, so that was part of me getting recognised. They might have thought they'd make a priest out of me up there too, but that never happened... they failed dismally there!

Farna won the Harty twice while I was there, in 1973 and '74, when we went on to win the All-Ireland colleges title, so that was three national medals that year. I came on to the senior panel in late 1975 for the Oireachtas Cup final against Wexford up in Croke Park and I was the only real 'new' fella on the panel in 1976, to a certain degree. Then in 1977, Tom Cashman, McCurtain and Fenton came on it. I had been under-21 in 1975 and '76, so there were a good few of that team moving up. I was very lucky to get on that team in 1976. You were playing alongside the likes of Charlie and Gerald McCarthy, Ray Cummins, Martin O'Doherty... some serious players.

I was playing wing-back and corner-back a lot of the time that year but then, before the All-Ireland final against Wexford, there was a reshuffle. John Horgan had been centre-back but he was replaced by Pat McDonnell from Inniscarra, who went full-back. Pat Barry went from full-back to right half-back and then I was told by Denis Murphy, who was a selector, that I'd be playing centre-back.

It was a bit of a shock! At the same time, I had no worries because I'd played centre-back at minor and for Farna, so it didn't faze me. We played a lot of backs and forwards in training and what you'd face from the Cork attackers would be as tough as anything you'd come across in a championship match. Kevin Kehilly, another West Cork man, was doing the physical training. People might look back and say that the training done wasn't as hard as now but, for the time, we were training at the optimal level.

After winning the three in-a-row as a young fella, you think that there's a bundle of it ahead of you at that stage but you're brought back to reality very quickly! The pressure was on at the start of 1984 but we had Justin McCarthy and Fr O'Brien as coaches and a very good backroom team. The Canon always wanted to be top dog, but Justin was a great coach.

The two of them were very good coaches in their own right, but Justin more so on the field. O'Brien was great for motivation and he had a good eye for hurling. He was dynamic in his own sense and he got the best out of fellas. I knew him from Farna and he had prior knowledge of so many of us as he had been the minor manager for six All-Ireland wins between 1969 and '79.

Justin was big into the hurling skills… and Noel Collins was involved too. He was out in Cork RTC at the time and he had new training methods. His methods brought us on that little bit again. It's like anything – you're always evolving when you're playing. You're learning from the next fella; from the younger fellas coming up and the older fellas above! It's a case of trying to pick up as much as you can – the day you stop learning is the day we're all in trouble!

I had played with Justin in 1975 for Seandún, the city divisional team, and he came out to Bishopstown coaching for a time too, so I had great time for him. He was still a great player and we got to the semi-final of the county championship in 1975, so that was probably another thing that had brought me into the fold. We had beaten the Barrs down in the Mardyke and Blackrock beat us in the semi-final and went on to win it after. He was great at the hurleys. He was meticulous – he'd shape them and round the bas, and change different things.

I still have the hurley that I played with in 1984.

The Munster final in 1984 was more pivotal than the All-Ireland, to a certain degree. Tipp were really up for it that time as they had been in the wilderness for a while and hadn't won the Munster Championship since 1971, but they had been successful at minor and under-21 so they were coming, as they proved later in the decade.

When they got the goal to go four points ahead, I thought we were beaten – I think we all did. One of their players running out gave me a shoulder and said, 'Ye're in trouble now!'… and we were a bit deflated, but within two minutes, the whole thing had changed again and that player got a belt in return. That's the way sport is! It was a very intense game and down to the wire. Seánie's goal, Lord have mercy on him, was integral to that.

We beat Antrim in the semi-final and that set up the final against Offaly – Cork's first time to play them in the championship. Offaly had won the All-Ireland in 1981 and when you look at their players, they had a lot of strong operators. They were a good team, a physical team and capable of strong running.

But, while we respected them, we still felt that we had a great chance ourselves as Thurles was like a home ground for us, to a certain degree. The public would have been even more confident and we went in as hot favourites but the hype was kept well away from us. Fr O'Brien and Justin did a great job that way.

We'd normally train the Monday or Tuesday night and finish up on the Thursday… you'd be told the team and it would be a fairly light session. You'd try to keep away from the chat as much as you could and not read the papers, though you'd generally come across them somewhere along the line! You tried not to take in too much and just concentrate on yourself, made sure you were right and that the gear was right… that you had the right hurley and spares and that everything was in order. In fairness to O'Brien, himself or Justin might ring for a chat, just to make sure everything was good. A lot of us were fairly experienced anyway and the younger fellas who had come in in the early 1980s were fairly clued-in, as well.

Normally, for an All-Ireland final you'd get the train up on the Saturday but because this one was in Thurles we didn't travel until the Sunday. It was great to be able to sleep in your own bed the night before.

It was a warm and humid day.

Going to the convent was a masterstroke by Fr O'Brien. We drove straight there and, while it's not half-a-mile from Thurles, it was very secluded. Nobody knew we were there – and even when Derry Gowen came to the door and asked to be let in, he was told we weren't there! It meant we could have the grub and a puck-around and that kept it very low-key for us. Normally we'd be up in the Anner Hotel and you'd be out on the green trying to puck-around and having hundreds watching us! It was like being apart from the whole thing, it kept us very grounded.

The talk for tickets beforehand was savage and people were told not to travel if they didn't have one – so a lot of people didn't… people who might normally have gone up to Dublin without one, hoping to get a ticket up there. Of course, what happened then was that there were people who had hoarded tickets and there was nobody to buy them!

When we got to Thurles and got off the bus outside the stadium, there was a garda with a bunch of tickets that people had given him in case anyone wanted one, but he couldn't give them away. There were still 50-odd thousand there, but they were just afraid that the whole thing would be over-run.

Brendan Bermingham was the guy who was centre-forward for Offaly. You'd know about these guys from having played against them previously and you might have seen them on the telly, but I wouldn't have gone into the nitty-gritty on the fella I'd be marking. I had Tom Cashman and Dermot McCurtain either side of me, two great wing-backs.

We had been playing together a while and we had a good understanding. Tom Cash was one of the best stick-players I'd ever played with, a great pair of wrists, and Dermot had good speed and for the size of him… he was tough as nails. So, even though they had a good half-forward line with Mark Corrigan and Pat Carroll on the wings, we had a formidable half-back line. We played well on the day, everybody came into the game at certain times – the work was distributed, as the fella says.

Overall, it was just a fierce relief as we had got back on the horse again. In fairness to Offaly, they lined up as we were coming out after and they clapped us out, which was a lovely touch. RTÉ had the outside broadcast unit there and, straight after the game, they were recording a piece for *The Sunday Game* that night, the Man of the Match and all that. Tony Sull got it and I still tell him I should have got it! After that, we went down to Dundrum House Hotel where there was a function there that night. There was a great camaraderie in that team... we celebrated well.

It was nice to win a fifth All-Ireland in 1986, but I retired after Tipp beat us in '87. I got an injury in the Munster final replay in Killarney – I broke my nose and got six stitches. That gets you thinking a bit! I got married in 1983 and our first daughter Claire was born in '84, after the All-Ireland. Things were moving on and there was a bigger commitment involved. I did go back training for a bit after that, but I made the call to retire.

I can't complain.

I had a great innings, with nine Munster Championships and five All-Irelands from seven finals. You look at fellas in the current crop and they haven't won any All-Ireland with Cork – luck comes into it as well, being in the right place at the right time... in the right year.

JIMMY BARRY-MURPHY

CORK 4-13 GALWAY 2-15
All-Ireland SHC Final
Croke Park
SEPTEMBER 7, 1986

Jimmy Barry-Murphy is blocked by Galway's Sylvie Linnane and Gerry McInerney during the 1986 All-Ireland final.

★ **CORK:** G Cunningham; D Mulcahy, R Browne, J Crowley; P Hartnett, T Cashman (0-1), D Walsh; J Fenton (1-4), J Cashman; T McCarthy, T Mulcahy (1-1), T O'Sullivan (0-1); G Fitzgerald (0-1), **J Barry-Murphy (0-2)**, K Hennessy (2-1). Subs: K Kingston (0-2) for Fenton.

★ **GALWAY:** J Commins (1-0); C Hayes, S Linnane, O Kilkenny; P Finnerty, T Keady (0-6), G McInerney; S Mahon (0-1), T Kilkenny; P Piggott, B Lynskey, M Naughton (0-2); A Cunningham, J Cooney (0-4), N Lane. Subs: PJ Molloy (1-1) for Piggott, M Connolly for Mahon, P Murphy (0-1) for Cunningham.

THE ACTION

WHILE GALWAY HAD a good record against Cork in recent All-Ireland semi-finals – winning in 1975, '79 and '85, compared to '77 and '83 for the Rebels – the three previous finals between the counties had gone the way of the Munster county.

The pre-match consensus was that Galway would never have a better chance to overcome Cork in a decider. They had been very impressive in beating Kilkenny in the All-Ireland semi-final, operating a three-man midfield, and much of the speculation centred around whether they would try a similar tactic against Cork, who only had five points to spare on Antrim in their semi-final.

Johnny Clifford's team had an early boost as John Fenton drilled an early free to the net. With Galway continuing with the tactic of keeping two men in the full-forward line, Johnny Crowley was able to mop up in the Cork defence while Teddy McCarthy – making his championship debut – showed no signs of being overawed. When Kevin Hennessy added a second goal, they were six points ahead.

However, the Rebels couldn't build on that early momentum and the long-range free-taking of Tony Keady helped Galway to claw their way back. By half-time, just a point separated the teams, with Cork leading by 2-5 to 0-10.

The game remained in the balance until the 48th minute, when Tomás Mulcahy scored a brilliant individual goal for Cork. When Hennessy scored his second and Cork's fourth on the hour-mark, they led by seven points. Though Galway goalkeeper John Commins did come up the field to net a 21-yard free two minutes later, Cork responded with points from captain Tom Cashman and sub Kieran Kingston.

PJ Molloy did score a late Galway goal after Ger Cunningham had saved from Tony Kilkenny. That cut the lead to three points, but Cork made sure of the win as Denis Walsh set up Jimmy Barry-Murphy for the final point of his last county game.

★★★★★

66

I THINK IT gradually came on me during 1986 that it would be my last year.

I was finding it hard to motivate myself and I think that the toll of playing for a good few years was something that was hitting me. My appetite was going, really, and I was tired from it, mentally more than anything else.

I did feel that my pace wasn't what it was and things like that, so as the year went on, I began to feel more and more that it would be my last.

I was relatively young, 32 at the time, but I'd been playing minor with Cork since 1971 and senior football from 1973 to '80.

I'm not making excuses, but it just all took a toll.

I was lucky to come into the Cork football team in 1973 and that had a big effect on me. I was influenced by a senior group of players on that football team, people like Billy Morgan, Frank Cogan, Ray Cummins – they had a huge impact on me in terms of attitude and working hard. I took a lot of examples from those lads, I learned an awful lot about the hard work that was needed to make it with Cork and stay there.

It was something I often looked back on.

The decision to concentrate on hurling after 1980 was a difficult one but, being selfish, Kerry were after becoming dominant and, I'm not going to tell lies, hurling looked to be a better prospect. I did feel that I had let the footballers down but it was a call that I had to make for myself.

I suppose making a decision to focus on hurling did at least give me a few more years than if I'd stayed playing both. I hated leaving the footballers and I often regretted the decision but it just wasn't physically possible to keep going with both.

I'd played eight years of senior football and both together since 1975, which was hard going.

I was minor in 1971 and '72. In 1971, we won the hurling All-Ireland and the football in '72 and lost the reverse finals each year. I was called on to the senior football panel in 1973, and we won the All-Ireland. It was 1975 that I made my senior hurling debut.

Justin McCarthy had come in as coach that year and he brought a new dimension to training and coaching, he was absolutely fantastic. The two wing-forwards that year were myself and Dinny Allen – Dinny was a very good hurler as well, he had a great year in 1975, and I often felt afterwards that he was very unlucky to miss out on the three in-a-row team... he should really have been a part of that.

We won the Munster title but lost to Galway in the All-Ireland semi-final, which was considered a shock, but we were beaten by a very good team on the day. There was a change after that and a new selection committee took over.

The three in-a-row was fantastic, obviously, and then the run came to an end with another defeat to Galway in 1979 – it's very hard to maintain such high standards indefinitely. We lost the finals to Kilkenny in 1982 and '83 and I was captain both years.

To lose both was tough, but sure, that's sport.

At the time, it was very disappointing but you just have to get up and get on with it. To win the All-Ireland in 1984 in Thurles was fantastic and I was delighted for John Fenton, it was great for him as he was a brilliant captain.

Justin and the Canon were in charge in 1984 and '85 but they stepped down after we lost the semi-final to Galway in '85. Johnny Clifford took over again – he had been in and out as a selector on the three in-a-row team and he had been there in 1983, too. The new selection committee for 1986 brought him in as coach; I was friendly with Johnny, so it was great to have him back involved.

By that time, there were very few of the lads from the 1970s left. Along with myself, there was only Johnny Crowley, really, and John Fenton had been on the panel. Johnny was a stalwart, an outstanding player.

Hurling was developing all the time. The time of the three in-a-row, it was very direct – one-dimensional, really – but by the mid-1980s there was more emphasis on the coaching side and the preparation. The physical training had become a bigger part of it.

I was lucky that all of the people who coached me over the years with Cork were of a fantastic calibre.

In 1986, we beat Clare in Killarney in the Munster final.

It was a very good game and it was my tenth Munster medal – I didn't realise it at the time, but I was equalling a record that John Doyle had held. I only read about it later but it's something nice to look back on.

We had a good team, so we didn't consider ourselves outsiders in the All-Ireland final against Galway, but I think most people did. We thought we had a great chance but they shocked a super Kilkenny team in Thurles, whereas we struggled to beat Antrim. The mantle of favouritism was always going to go on Galway and that suited us... it often did.

We were struggling with injuries too.

John Hodgins was out injured and so was Dermot McCurtain. John Fenton was carrying an injury but, thank God, he started. Then you had a new breed of player coming through – Denis Walsh came into the team that year and he had an outstanding game at left half-back for a guy playing in his first final, and Kieran Kingston came on and got a vital score.

It was Teddy McCarthy's first final, too – he had been on the fringes of the team all year and missed the semi-final, but he was brought in for the final and played very well. You'd all those new lads coming through and it was very exciting from that point of view.

I had been in the half-forwards in the 1970s but from 1983 on, I was almost always in the full-forward line and never really ventured out of that area!

My game had changed in that I wasn't doing as much running – not that I ever did a lot, anyway! – but full-forward was my favourite position... I loved it. It was a very strong forward unit and everyone worked well together. I had some great players around me and that always makes it easier.

I found that I got more nervous ahead of big games as I came to the end of my career – the pressure gets to you a bit more, especially after losing in 1982 and '83.

Thankfully, we got a good start in the 1986 final and that was a huge help. Obviously, playing in a lot of finals means you're familiar with the rhythms of the weekend and the day itself, but it doesn't make it any easier.

The nerves are stronger as you get older, there's no doubt about that. I didn't have a care in the world playing in my first few finals, it didn't faze me at all!

I always enjoyed the greyhounds, and going to Shelbourne Park on the Sunday night had become part of the routine. A few of the lads – Ger Cunningham, Tomás Mul, Kevin Hennessy – used to come with me to pass away a few hours... then back to the hotel and bed early. A few other lads used to go to the cinema –

players need to have some distraction. Later, when I was manager, we used to do something together, the whole group would go to a show or something.

Sunday morning always felt drawn-out.

You're up early for your breakfast but then you're hanging around for a few hours. Cork were playing in the minor final that year and we watched a good bit of that in the hotel before we left – unfortunately, they were beaten that day by Offaly.

Sylvie Linnane was marking me.

Conor Hayes was in the full-back line as well and I thought it might have been him, but Conor played in the right corner.

We all knew each other well and would have played against each other a good bit – we were a seasoned team and so were they. I found that Galway were a great team and Cyril Farrell was an absolutely brilliant manager. He was ahead of his time, really; he was very innovative and tried different tactics and things.

He and Galway got their reward when they won in 1987 and '88 – I got to know him properly later and he was an absolute gentleman.

One of their tactical innovations was to go with a third midfielder against Kilkenny and we weren't sure what to do if they tried that again against us. Ultimately, they did and the decision was that Johnny Crowley would stay in the corner and it proved to be the right one. He was absolutely brilliant in the role, read the game brilliantly and ended up getting Man of the Match – though we always slag him about winning the award for marking nobody!

We got a 21-yard free early on and John Fenton took everybody by surprise by going for it… and burying it. John was his own man and if he felt there was a chance, he'd go for it. It really took Galway by surprise and gave us the confidence that we needed. Then Kevin got a brilliant goal soon after and that gave us a great cushion.

We led for much of the game, but we were still never fully sure of the victory. We were up by six and they got a goal to bring it back to three again, but then Denis Walsh won a brilliant ball and passed it to me and I got the insurance point. That was a fantastic feeling.

I knew we were there then.

I had decided to pack up by then, so it was a nice way to go out.

I had great friends on the team and we were all so close for many years. I was great friends with Johnny Clifford and Jimmy Brohan, who was a selector, and Dónal O'Grady was a selector that year too, having played with us in 1984.

When I started off with the Barrs, I was only thinking about playing senior hurling and football for the club, that was my only ambition. But then, that graduates to playing minor for Cork and playing on the senior team. To have done that in hurling and football was a dream come true.

JOHN CONSIDINE
(GER FITZGERALD & TONY O'SULLIVAN)

CORK 4-16 TIPPERARY 2-14
Munster SHC Final
Semple Stadium
JULY 16, 1990

Stopping Tipperary from winning four Munster titles in-a-row in 1990 carried John Considine and Cork to the All-Ireland final and the opportunity of being one part of an historic double act.

★ **CORK:** G Cunningham; **J Considine**, D Walsh, S O'Gorman; S McCarthy, J Cashman, K McGuckin; P Buckley, B O'Sullivan; D Quirke (0-1), M Foley (2-7), **T O'Sullivan (0-5)**; **G Fitzgerald (0-1)**, K Hennessy (0-1), J Fitzgibbon (2-0). Subs: A O'Sullivan for Quirke, C Casey (0-1) for Buckley.

★ **TIPPERARY:** K Hogan; J Madden, N Sheehy, B Ryan; Conal Bonnar, J Kennedy, P Delaney; D Carr, J Hayes; M Cleary (1-5), Declan Ryan (0-1), C Stakelum (0-2); P Fox, J Leahy (0-2), N English (1-4). Subs: Dinny Ryan for Fox, Colm Bonnar for Carr.

THE ACTION

FIRST OFF, LET us try to offer a defence of Michael 'Babs' Keating. The Tipperary manager is (dis)credited with having said, 'Donkeys don't win derbies' in relation to Cork's chances of beating his side, who were the reigning All-Ireland champions. In fact, he was praising the Rebels.

Keating did an interview with RTÉ's Ger Canning on the Tuesday before the Munster final, broadcast on *Sports Stadium* on the Saturday and his love of horseracing led him to use a metaphor that went on to be misunderstood by so many. Canning asked, 'Of course, you have to respect a team motivated and trained by people like Fr Michael O'Brien and Gerald McCarthy?' Keating's reply to that was, 'You still need the talent, you still need the players. Several managers in recent weeks got credit for being great motivators but if you have not the talent...you can't win a derby with a donkey'.

What Keating meant was that it didn't matter who Cork's manager was if they didn't have good players, and those players backed up that assessment with a performance full of craft and graft, with 2-7 from Mark Foley the centrepiece.

Tipp were aiming to complete a Munster four in-a-row for the first time since 1952, but Cork – despite being without injured captain Tomás Mulcahy and Teddy McCarthy – never let them dictate matters. Tony O'Sullivan's point had the visitors ahead inside 50 seconds and, with Jim Cashman dominant at centre-back and Brendan O'Sullivan strong in midfield, they led by three after 27 minutes.

However, Michael Cleary levelled for Tipp with a goal, before John Leahy and Nicky English added points. English's goal suggested that the pre-match expectations might be proven right. Cork weren't ruffled though and, when Foley diverted a sideline cut from stand-in captain Kieran McGuckin to the net, they went in trailing by just two points, 2-5 to 1-6.

After O'Sullivan levelled with a pair of points on the restart, English put Tipp back in front but it was the last time they led – O'Sullivan set up John Fitzgibbon for a goal and Cork had managed to push six clear by the 50th minute. While Tipp came back again to cut the lead to a single point with eight minutes left, a point from Foley, followed by his second goal, eased Cork worries.

★★★★★

66

ONE OF MY little things was that I used to like to run out onto the field behind the captain, second in the line.

Tomás Mulcahy was our captain for 1990, but he was injured for the Munster final and so Kieran McGuckin was the captain that day as he was the next in line from Glen Rovers. The Glen had beaten my club Sarsfields in the county final and, if we had won, Teddy McCarthy would have been captain – but he was injured too.

So, I was running out behind Kieran and I remember thinking that, because Teddy was out, I'd have been captain if we'd won the county final.

I'm not sure if I'd have been able to handle it!

I was old making my championship debut against Kerry in 1990, a few months short of my 26th birthday. I was born on October 26, which is obviously very late in the year and there's a lot of stuff out there that says that most fellas who go on to play at elite level, particularly at underage, are born at the start of the year.

I got a trial as a minor in 1982. That was on out in Buttevant and I was centre-back but Kieran Kingston, the centre-forward against me, gave me a roasting. I won primary possession most of the time but his hooking and blocking was something I'd never come across before – in the first-half alone, there must have been four balls that I won, but he hooked me and took it off me.

I didn't make it.

It was a straight knockout format in the championship at that time and Cork were beaten by Tipperary in their first game. That was on a Wednesday, and on the Friday evening I made my senior hurling club debut for Sars against St Finbarr's. I played well enough in that and if Cork had progressed, I might have made it back – who knows, but I didn't. Coaching Sars that year was Fr Michael O'Brien, so I might have at least laid some foundation for the future.

The following year, 1983, I went from not being on the minor side to being on the extended panel for the under-21s. I was actually on the under-21 squad for three years without ever playing.

You know the way in American sports how they'll retire the jersey of a really good player? My club colleague Tadhg Murphy used to joke that Cork were going to retire the No 25 in honour of me… no feelings spared!

I played a challenge game against Galway in 1986 for the seniors, and I got bits and pieces of league games in 1988 but, until you're picked for the championship, you don't really know how you're rated. UCC was one element of my progress, winning Fitzgibbon Cups under the Canon – though I didn't go straight to college after my Leaving Cert, I worked for four years – and Sars getting to the county final in 1989 was a plus, even though we were beaten by the Glen. I was in that shop window and if I hadn't been, then I probably wouldn't have got the opportunity.

I was even lucky in how the schedule worked.

The league in those days was over the winter and spring, and I was picked for a game against Galway in October 1989, not long after the county final – the first one in charge for the Canon and Gerald McCarthy. I did well enough, though they had brought in some experimental rules and one was that you couldn't kick the ball out of your hands… and I broke that one!

I got injured then for another game and Kevin Cashman – an uncle of John Fitzgibbon's – wrote in the *Irish Independent* that my injury was a blessing for Cork because, even though I had played well in the first two games, come the summer there was no way I'd be able to mark Pat Fox or Nicky English.

When you're young, you think it's great fun people saying those things!

After the break, I played against Kilkenny and did okay but then, for the last game away to Limerick, they brought Brendan O'Sullivan back to corner-back. I thought… *This is it, back to the old days where I play a few league games and I'm not trusted for championship.*

I can understand it in a way, as I had no underage pedigree.

We qualified for the league semi-final against Wexford and, again, I wasn't started. Christy Connery from Na Piarsaigh was in one corner, Bryan Murphy from Bishopstown – who later played football for Kildare – was full-back and Denis Walsh was in the other corner. That game turned out to be a draw… and Bryan Murphy got injured.

As well as that – unfairly, I felt, but it worked out well for me – Christy Connery was blamed for a Wexford goal. He turned back towards the goal to look for a pass and was dispossessed, and the ball ended up in the net. I think he paid the price for that with his place for the replay.

We played the replay up in Nowlan Park on Easter Monday and I was thrown in for Christy. Seán O'Gorman, full-forward in the drawn game, was back at full-back instead of Bryan, who had torn his hamstring.

You talk about the way things go for you… Wexford were well on top and I was marking Tom Dempsey, so there was a lot of ball down our way and I did well. That's how I got in, essentially.

If there had been no draw the first day, I probably wouldn't have.

My first championship game was against Kerry and, in many ways, it wasn't much of a thing, but it was a huge deal for me as I was getting on to the field. They had a guy called John Hennessy, who had been a replacement All Star the previous year – the All-Ireland champions would play the All Stars and the places on the All Star team that the champions had won would be filled by guys from other counties. He was their main man and I was marking him.

I was in bonus-land… I was just delighted to play against Kerry, rather than looking at it and getting worried. We won, and in the Munster semi-final against Waterford I won ball after ball. Then, you get to the Munster final against Tipp in Thurles… but that's a different animal.

In those days, you didn't get a bus… instead, we used to get hackneys. The old road to Dublin went through Glanmire and Riverstown, so Teddy McCarthy – who was out injured – selector Denis Hurley and I would go to Riverstown Cross, where we'd be picked up. The Cork traffic heading up early, flags out the window and everything, would recognise Teddy… they'd beep as they were driving past.

Mentally, I was still half a supporter, so there was all that kind of excitement on the way up!

We'd meet up then at the Anner Hotel outside Thurles, where we'd have soup and sandwiches. Nowadays, the idea of having bread before a game would be frowned upon, but I think some of that stuff has gone overboard.

After that, we'd have a team meeting, but we'd be out and about and people would know Cork were there… there'd be people over having chats. It was great, in a way, all very relaxed as the excitement was building.

Then you're ready to go up the town… and that's when it kind of struck me.

We got back into the cars and drove up – no garda escort or anything like that. Again, people would look in and see Teddy, so they'd be roaring into the car…

'Go on Cork!' Or the Tipp lads would be saying they'd beat us. It was amazing, though… literally driving through the crowd! It was a great experience.

Eventually, we got to the ground and got ready and all of that, and it was time to go out. We turned right, down to the Town End, where the Cork support was. I'm not joking, I can still nearly feel the hairs rising on the back of my neck as I think of it. It was brilliant… amazing stuff. I was down to mark Nicky English, who had been Hurler of The Year in 1989.

The Canon had obviously coached Nicky for some of UCC's eight Fitzgibbon Cup wins in-a-row, but all he said in the team meeting was, 'There's a lot of talk about their full-forward line and who's able for this and who's able for that… we've picked players and we've every confidence in them'.

The late Paul O'Connor, who was also on those Fitz teams and was on our panel, had said to me – looking back, I think it was through the Canon, but I'm only speculating – that English had been on to him to find out about me, but I think that might have been to build my confidence. As it turned out, I was only on him for 25 minutes. He was actually switched and went in full-forward on Denis Walsh.

I did okay and the reason I say that is because there wasn't much ball that came our way, and much of the ball that did come, I got it away. Any ball he got, he was outside me… and I kept him out.

Michael Cleary came on to me and I'd been on him before, so I was used to him. Cormac Bonnar didn't play – people reckoned, I don't know how true it was, that Tipp were preparing for a potential All-Ireland final against Galway and they weren't going to put a big man on the Galway full-back Conor Hayes.

They brought on Dinny Ryan and, again, it just shows how delighted I was to be playing – he came over to me and I just shook his hand… no shoulder or anything.

The way I saw it was… it was a new half and a new player.

I was just concerned about playing, focusing on what I was doing. It was only halfway through the second-half that I considered what was happening. We were playing the All-Ireland champions and we were big outsiders, so it was a big shock in some ways.

At that stage, an 'Olé… Olé, Olé, Olé!' chant went up from the Cork terrace, though afterwards, Mark Foley said he thought they were saying, 'Fol-ey… Fol-ey!'

When that chant started, I remember thinking... *Holy shit, we're actually going to win this!* I had got the butt of a hurley into my nether regions – totally accidental, there was a coming together – so there was a little pain from that, but otherwise I was feeling as comfortable as can be in a game like that.

We had a big lead... the sun was shining, we're in Thurles.

It was heaven.

Afterwards, we had to walk back up through the crowd to the Anner.

It felt excellent. It was just contentment... I certainly wasn't thinking about the All-Ireland or anything like that. Here I was, third championship game... never been beaten. I thought this was easy stuff! There was no downside. I wasn't a young player, but I was an inexperienced one and this was all just amazingly new.

I was lucky in that I'd Ger Cunningham behind me, and Denis Walsh and Seán O'Gorman were in the full-back line too, so there was experience there. Okay, Seánie McCarthy was another newbie outside me, but Jim Cashman at centre-back had played in 1986 as well. This is where I think the lads in the current era have a tougher time.

I grew up at a time when Cork were regularly winning All-Irelands – I was in secondary school for the three in-a-row, and I was up there watching in 1986.

The feeling was... *We're Cork, why shouldn't we win?*

I wasn't worried about any of that side of things, I was just focused on my own game and enjoying the ride... *This is great stuff.*

I always talk about being lucky.

Things fell for me with the Fitzgibbon, with Sars (even though we didn't win the county) and the league going well for me. And yet, with all that going for me, I still needed us to draw the first league semi-final against Wexford to get in.

It even fell well for me in that, because we were under pressure in the replay, I got a lot of ball and I could play well. Sometimes, you play in a game where you're well on top... and you do nothing!

If you look at the way I got my introduction to the championship, there was Kerry and then Waterford, so it was building... and then on to Tipp. Everything fell into place.

I often see where people say that everything about their success is down to themselves or whatever, but – while you do have to do all the stuff yourself, don't get me wrong – you need to get lucky, too. It was my first year and we won an All-Ireland.

The following year, a young fella called Brian Corcoran comes on to the panel as a teenager and it took him eight years to win one! It just happens… you catch the wave. I was lucky enough to do that that year.

I won an All Star that year, but again, I'd say I got it because of who I was marking. I gave away five points from play in the championship, but there was good fortune involved. Like I said, I was marking John Hennessy and then English; we played Antrim in the All-Ireland semi-final and I was on Olcan McFetridge, who had been one of Antrim's best players the previous year.

Then, in the final, I was marking Galway's Éanna Ryan, and not a whole lot of ball came our way. There was an incident in that match where I second-guessed, I went out to the ball and I was going to pull but, at the last second, I reckoned he'd hook me.

I stuck the hurley in the ground, but the ball went over it. I turned to see him picking it up and heading for goal. I was thinking… *I'm in trouble here!*

Fortunately, he stuck it over the bar rather than going for goal.

In 1984, I had been up in the Town End for the All-Ireland final in Thurles. In 1988, I was on the extended panel, so I was one of the fellas carrying the hurleys for the Munster semi-final against Clare, but I wasn't part of it for the final. I was on the terrace in the Gaelic Grounds. So, I was literally a fan having jumped the wire for 1990.

I would have idolised a lot of those players and the only thing that kept me sane was the fact that I had played with Teddy for Sars. *He's one of the best players in Ireland… if I can get close to him, I can manage.* I was in awe of so many of those fellas and then, all of a sudden, I'm playing on the same team as them so I was delighted with life.

I remember the match but I wasn't central to it.

As a corner-back, you're rarely more than 40 yards from your own goal, so you're seeing the stuff in front of you but it's more about minding your patch and staying on guard. It was just enough for me – like I say, if I was captain I might have been overwhelmed.

If you were a manager now, you'd be worried about a fella like me, that he mightn't be tuned in enough.

I wasn't playing the occasion, but I was *enjoying* the occasion.

There's a huge nervous energy there, but you're watching other fellas because you've never seen any of this before. You're taking your cues from them.

If we had been beaten, it could have been a harrowing experience… I don't know. But it just went well… everything fell into place.

I know how lucky I got.

GER FITZGERALD

Ger Fitzgerald rounds Bobby Ryan during the epic Munster final clash against Tipperary in 1990.

❝

YOU'VE HEARD OF the phrase, 'Flying in training?'

Well in 1990, I was flying *to* training!

I was working for Aer Lingus in Dublin Airport at the time and I was flying up and down for training, twice or three times a week, depending on what was required.

I'd come down and my mother Liz would collect me at the airport and drop me to training... back up the next morning and back to work. She had been around the block with the inter-county scene, as my father Paddy played for Cork – he was part of the successful 1966 panel. She was now doing the same with her son.

It was brilliant to be able to get down for training, though! I used to do gym work on my own up in Dublin, too. Cork did a lot of training in Ballinlough in the lead-up to the Munster final because Páirc Uí Chaoimh was being used for a *Prince* concert. Because of the nature of the pitch – it's very tight – it made the training very intense and the games were fairly robust.

I remember a couple of hardy backs-and-forwards sessions!

I was on the panel since 1984, on and off, and a regular fixture from '85. We had won the All-Ireland in 1986, my first year playing championship, really. Then, after that, we were beaten by Tipperary in 1987 after a replay, and in '88 they beat us in Limerick.

In 1989, I was on and off the panel and I wasn't there for the match against Waterford. Tomás wasn't on it, either. They made a lot of changes going into that game, which was fair enough – they were entitled to that.

The 1986 final was really the end of a team that won five Munster Championships in-a-row, won two All-Irelands and reached two other finals. John Fenton, Tom Cashman, Jimmy Barry-Murphy, Johnny Crowley... they were coming to the end of their time and there was a heap of us starting off... players like Denis Walsh, Jim Cashman, myself, Teddy Mac.

It was our first year, really, playing championship hurling.

There was a lot of excitement around the Tipp replay in 1987 given that they hadn't won Munster in so long and, after that, they went on to dominate for a while. They were a good team, well-organised. They brought in Babs and they had a bit of a structure about themselves.

At the end of 1989 there was a management change and there was a big effort put into the National League. We trained pretty hard. Gerald McCarthy was the trainer and he did a very good job. Sometimes, you wouldn't do much training before Christmas, but we did; it was pretty tough from the start because we knew we needed to pick things up. We were after slipping off the pace a little bit.

I had been on the fringes of the panel in 1984, so I had experience of working with the Canon. He was a great guy at getting into fellas' heads. You also knew that there was going to be a good structure around the team.

Frank Murphy was on board as a selector, too, which was always a big help – things were that little bit easier to access because of that! At the time, it was certainly a significant addition, because there was less bartering with the County Board for access to things. It was all that little bit smoother.

We were beaten in the league semi-final by Wexford in Nowlan Park. After a pretty good campaign, we played poorly in the semi-final itself. They beat us well. It was a cold, miserable day and we just didn't play well.

So, much and all as we were positive during the league, we came out of that a bit dejected.

After the Wexford game, we went away and played a couple of practice matches then and just tried to get going for the championship. The weather improved and we started doing a bit more hurling training and that made a big difference to us.

We had been drawn against Kerry in Tralee and it turned out to be a tough ould match!

We won easily enough in the end, but for 45 minutes it was difficult. Kerry scored three goals against us and nobody else managed that in that year's championship. They played well, but then they had good players – Christy Walsh was a serious player, for instance, he could have played on a lot of county teams.

For the semi-final, we had Waterford in Thurles and it was a serious match, given what had happened in 1989. We knew how tough it would be and we were well-focused. We had to up our game and be better than we had been against Kerry but I think that Kerry game helped us… just getting a run-out in the championship.

We played so well that day that it gave us a lot of confidence going into the final against Tipp, but in the meantime we had picked up a couple of injuries – Tomás got injured and so did Teddy. Tony O'Sullivan had been out for the Waterford match, so we were blooding fellas, as much out of necessity as anything. The panel was being extended a little bit.

With those injuries, the pressure was off us in a way going in to face Tipp. In fairness, when you're playing Tipp in Thurles, it's always a huge challenge, anyway – it's a great venue and the atmosphere is brilliant.

Our own preparation was pretty decent. Fair enough, we had the few injuries, but the lads who had come in – David Quirke, Anthony O'Sullivan from Bishopstown – did well and Kieran McGuckin was a superb stand-in captain for Tomás.

We had the core of a good team, and the Canon was a great fella to motivate guys. The Babs thing?

I think there was a lot made of it after. In fairness to him, he was never a man to be shy about public utterances! He left a hostage to fortune there which came back to haunt him. In terms of whether or not it improved us on the day? I would say it had nothing to do with it, really.

We were in a good position.

We were well-prepared and we were primed.

It started off dampish. I was in corner-forward and I was marking Bobby Ryan. You'd be watching the fella who you'd be up against and I had six-stud boots on and I noticed he had multi-studs. Particularly in the first half, the surface was wet and you know that if you turn a fella fast, he wouldn't be as quick to get you.

Small little things like that give you a bit of an edge and a bit of confidence.

Tipp were raging-hot favourites and, in fairness to them, they had a serious team when you look at those players. They had a right to be favourites, given that we didn't have a lot of form. In saying that, we still had eight or nine of the team that won the All-Ireland in 1986. There wasn't a lot of notice taken of that but I think that was significant in that a good few of us had been through the mill, and knew the craic. We were experienced, without getting the acknowledgement for that before the match.

I suppose there was a bit of complacency with Tipperary, that would be fair to say, but at the same time they did start the game fairly well and it took us a while to get into it.

The longer we stayed in it, the more confident we got and Mark got a great goal just before half-time to give us a significant boost going in. We were well in the hunt.

In 1988, they got ahead of us early and they dominated, but we were well in the game and we were playing pretty decent. We were competitive all over the field, our defence was good. They had a vaunted forward line with Fox, English, Michael Cleary, Declan Ryan… but our backs were doing well. We were playing reasonably well as a team and we knew that we were well in with a shout.

Fitzy got two goals and Foley got another one, and that made a massive difference. When you're playing a game like that and you get goals, confidence grows. It was a tough match to the end but we hurled very well as a team and we came of age as a group that day, I think.

If you looked at it, five of the six forwards would have been noted goal-scorers... you had Kevin, Fitzy, Mul, myself and Foley... and Sully would be the only fella who'd hit it over the bar! To be fair to him, he was prolific at that and he had a very good game in the Munster final.

It was the game that made Mark. To be fair to him, he had come through the system; he played minor and under-21. That team was built on the core of lads who played in 1986 and then the lads who played under-21 in '88 – Foley, Fitzy, Cathal Casey. There was a backbone of success and a very capable group of hurlers.

The significance of that victory was that it opened up the door to the All-Ireland. We knew we had Antrim, and Tomás Mul and Teddy were coming back after their injuries, so there was a natural competition for places anyway.

Having not been in an All-Ireland final in a couple of years, we didn't want to make a mess of the semi-final against Antrim.

It was a relatively toughish game, without being put to the pin of our collar. It was good to get into Croke Park, get familiar with the situation and build more confidence. You'd be expected to win it, but they had been in the previous year's All-Ireland final and they had beaten Offaly as well.

We were well aware what they were capable of, because they had run us close in 1986, as well. In terms of a crowd, it was as close as what you'd get during the pandemic... there was nobody there, really!

They could be a banana skin, but we played well and we beat them. That put us up against Galway again and they had won two in-a-row since we beat them in 1986.

They were a very good team, they had been dominating with Tipp, but we wouldn't have been lacking in confidence taking them on, either.

TONY O'SULLIVAN

At the end of the long and thrilling summer of 1990, Tony O'Sullivan celebrates with teammates on the steps of the Hogan Stand.

"

WE WERE GOING in as huge underdogs for the Munster final because Tipp had an amazing team at the time, but we had our homework done and we were very quiet about it. We said it to nobody but we were quietly confident.

All of the pressure was on them.

We needed a good start, and got a good start, and the thing about it is that we were down two huge players in Teddy Mac and Tomás. It was a huge occasion for us but we picked up a few scores early on.

They came back at us but we pushed on again and it was actually a great performance... nobody was expecting it except ourselves.

I played my first championship match for Cork in 1982 against Tipperary... we won and carried on. We had a great year that year. I was playing with the likes of Tim Crowley, Seánie O'Leary and Ray Cummins, and you couldn't go wrong with the likes of those guys.

We were beaten in the 1982 and '83 finals, which was disappointing, but to go on and win it then in '84, the centenary final, was huge for us.

I started all of 1982 but then in '83 I got sick, and I was out for a while.

I came on in the final alright, but I wasn't at full fitness. I didn't play a lot of hurling in 1983 but I was back again in '84. It was a case of the pressure being on, you know how it is in Cork, but to be fair, we put huge work into it. We had an exceptional team and we were probably well over Offaly in the final.

That year's Munster final was just as pivotal. I came on and got a goal, and then we got another one. I hit a ball that was going over the bar, but John Sheedy brought it down and Seánie stuck it. It was an incredible finish to the game and it gave us a new lease of life.

We had a great few years, from 1982 up to '86, where we won all the Munster finals. Carrying on from that, we lost to Tipp down in Killarney in 1987 and fell back a bit then in '88 and '89. We had a disaster in 1989 against Waterford – basically, we weren't really organised, with due respect.

A few of us – the older stock – had got together and had a couple of meetings.

We said we were after letting ourselves down… letting the public down, our clubs down in 1988 and '89, so it was a case that we needed to get things back together.

I must say, it was one of the hardest times we ever worked with Cork.

The whole lot. We needed to get back on the road and the Canon and Gerald Mac were there, there was a huge impetus.

In 1980, I was a student in North Monastery and we won the Dr Harty Cup and the All-Ireland colleges title. I was in Leaving Cert and we only celebrated the 40th anniversary of that two years ago. That was the start of it.

The GAA side of it was a huge thing in the Mon. The tradition was there and the minute you got inside the door, you were involved in it. To go on and win it was a huge thing for us. Dónal O'Grady and Murt Murphy were involved with us. Dónal was brilliant, he brought us to a new level.

We won the Harty after a replay against Colman's and then we went on to play Birr of Offaly in the All-Ireland final. I was actually marking Ken Hogan – who would go on to play in goal for Tipperary – that day.

I was full-forward and he was full-back. We had a very good team…Tomás Mul was there and Paul O'Connor, from own club Na Piarsaigh, who tragically died in 2012.

From the Féile up, Piarsaigh won pretty much everything – under-16 county, minor hurling and football counties, a couple of under-21 counties. A lot of the fellas who won the Harty would have been involved – it was just an exceptional team.

The club was progressing at the time. It was strong and we had a lot of good players there together at the same time. It was just one of those things.

After the Harty in 1980, I played a bit of minor with Cork and the first time I played with the senior team was a National League game down the Páirc against Galway.

I was going down and was sitting alongside Ray Cummins and all these fellas. I played one game before Christmas, in November, because we were still stuck in county championships at underage.

When you're young like that, you'd be conscious of trying to make the step up but, in fairness, the lads were brilliant to me when I started off that time, in particular Johnny Crowley. He'd have been a friend of ours, he was going out with a girl in the club and he looked after me and brought me through, but every one of them was brilliant.

By 1990, I was one of the more experienced guys and we felt that we had to come with a strong response. Things changed around because a lot of players decided to get going again when the new management came in. We had been going since 1982, so we were pushing on a bit and we were fortunate that there were a few younger fellas coming through at that stage.

There was a good balance there.

We beat Kerry and Waterford, and we were going to Thurles to face Tipp, knowing that we were fit and that we were hurling well… but we said nothing about it.

The Canon had been involved with Justin in 1984. I obviously went to the Mon rather than Farna and I didn't go to the College, so the only other time that

I'd have played under him was when we won the All-Ireland minor in 1979 – I was still only under-16, at the time.

The Canon's speeches before games and his passion for it couldn't be replicated. You couldn't not buy into his passion, the way he got everybody going. Everything was coming together – we had the management and we were after working hard.

Gerald brought *Gerald Mac* to it, if that makes sense.

Everything had been lethargic for a couple of years before that and we needed to speed up our play. We needed a whole change-around. At the end of the day, we were all able to hurl, that wasn't going to be a problem at all.

It was just a case of smartening up our hurling.

In terms of superstitions, for some particular reason, for photographs I always sat at the front, at the right-hand side. I don't know what it was, these stupid things… it was actually pointed out to me by other people.

I wasn't bothered where I sat in the dressing-room or anything like that.

At the end of the day, I loved playing in Thurles, it was a great sod.

Babs' perceived comments? We didn't ever worry about that. He's a very respected man in Cork and in GAA circles. We would be great friends with the Tipperary players because of all of the Munster finals we played.

There's something special about Cork and Tipp.

That day, there was a huge crowd but no pressure on us… all of the pressure was on Tipp. Jim Cashman had a blinder and everybody contributed – okay, Mark Foley was exceptional on the day, but a few of the older fellas needed to stand up too and I was delighted with my performance, scoring five points from play. David Quirke had a great game that day, so did Pat Buckley. Everybody chipped in with scores – myself, Ger Fitzgerald, Kevin Hennessy… and then John Fitzgibbon, he was always going to get a couple of goals.

It's all about panels and everybody contributing, that's it. From January, we were back and everybody knuckled down. Things don't come together unless you work hard and get organised, and it was just one of those years where things worked out for us.

It was the same in the All-Ireland final against Galway.

Again, we were underdogs, but Cork never feared anyone in a final.

We were shocking in the first-half that day, but we came back and it all just boiled down to hard work. We never put in so much as we did that time. It wasn't really an exceptional team but it was full of grafters.

The year got even better then when Na Piarsaigh won the county Senior Hurling Championship. It was our first one, a huge occasion for us and it brought the club to a new level. It was the same thing in terms of the hard work – obviously, we had a great coach in Eamonn Ryan and all of these things make a difference.

We were playing St Finbarr's in the final and they were an excellent team, too – we needed a replay to win it It's so hard to win any county title, but it's even harder to win your first one. We knew at some stage, with the team that we had and the talent that we had, that we needed to win one.

You don't know when these opportunities are going to come around again and, thankfully, we took ours. To cap it off, I won an All Star… and Hurler of The Year.

SEÁN O'GORMAN
(& TOMÁS MULCAHY)

CORK 5-15 GALWAY 2-21
All-Ireland SHC Final
Croke Park
SEPTEMBER 2, 1990

Seán O'Gorman is presented to the crowd on All-Ireland final day in 2015, as part of the jubilee celebrations of Cork's triumph over Galway 25 years earlier.

★ **CORK:** G Cunningham; J Considine, D Walsh, **S O'Gorman**; S McCarthy, J Cashman, K McGuckin (0-1); B O'Sullivan, T McCarthy (0-3); G Fitzgerald (0-1), M Foley (1-1), T O'Sullivan (0-2); **T Mulcahy (1-2)**, K Hennessy (1-4), J Fitzgibbon (2-1). Subs: D Quirke for McGuckin, C Casey for B O'Sullivan.

★ **GALWAY:** J Commins; D Fahy, S Treacy, O Kilkenny; P Finnerty, T Keady (0-1), G McInerney; M Coleman (0-1), P Malone; A Cunningham (0-1), J Cooney (1-7, 2f), M Naughton (0-4); M McGrath (0-1), N Lane (0-4), É Ryan (0-2). Subs: T Monaghan for Malone, B Lynskey (1-0) for Cunningham.

THE ACTION

AT HALF-TIME, it looked for all the world as if Galway would end their final hoodoo against Cork; when a five-point lead was extended to seven on the resumption, Cork's pre-game status as underdogs seemed all the more understandable.

Though Cork had a goal from Kevin Hennessy after 48 seconds and they led until the 19th minute, Galway looked likelier champions when they got on top. The Tribesmen's captain Joe Cooney was in inspired form in the first-half, while Tony Keady at centre-back and midfielder Michael Coleman were also to the fore.

Cooney's kicked goal levelled the game at 1-6 each, before Éanna Ryan put Cyril Farrell's side ahead for the first time in the 20th minute and they drove on from there. After one Cooney point, Cork centre-back Jim Cashman banged his hurley to the ground in frustration as if to say, *What can I do here?* But Galway wasted at least two good goal chances and, though Cork turned with a deficit of 1-13 to 1-8, they were not a lost cause by any means.

After Cork squandered goal opportunities early in the second-half, Galway added two more points to buttress their lead, but a superb goal by Cork captain Tomás Mulcahy in the 44th minute – running on to a Ger Cunningham clearance – suggested there was momentum to be mined by the men in red. When Cunningham then bravely saved from Martin Naughton – injuring his nose – and the ball was waved wide rather than a '65' being awarded, the feeling was amplified.

Mulcahy at centre-forward broke Tony Keady's grip and, at the other end, Cashman began to get the upper-hand on Cooney, while Seán O'Gorman was excellent in defence. They had drawn to within two points by the time Mark Foley found the net and, though Galway drew level again, John Fitzgibbon raised the green flag twice in quick succession.

Galway sub Brendan Lynskey did get a second goal for them to ensure that the outcome wasn't decided until the very end, but Cork held out. A fortnight later, the county's football team beat Meath to secure the only 'double' of the modern era.

★★★★★

66

EVERYTHING I EVER won at county level with Cork, the Canon – or the Archdeacon, to give him his proper title at the time of his death – was involved.

We lost the All-Ireland minor final to Kilkenny in 1977, after a replay. They had beaten Waterford in the Munster semi-final and I wasn't even in the squad but there was a trial match in Páirc Uí Chaoimh before the final against Limerick, and I was called for that.

I was playing full-back or corner-back and at half-time the Canon, who was over the team with Tom Nott from Na Piarsaigh and Paddy O'Mahony from Inniscarra, asked me if I'd consider playing full-forward for the second-half.

I said, 'No bother, I'll go up!' And I can't remember exactly what happened but I did well enough and, next thing, I was picked full-forward for the Limerick game. I scored four points and we won by one.

The next year, I was full-forward again and we won the All-Ireland against Kilkenny. I played three years under-21 and I was actually captain for the first of those in 1979 as Milford had won the county under-21 in '78 as well. We were beaten in three Munster finals in-a-row by Tipperary.

Milford were on the up at the time.

We won the county junior in 1981, having hardly even won a North Cork title for around 40 years! We were lucky to beat St Catherine's by a point in the county final. They were trained by Denis Coughlan of the Glen and Denis Walsh was playing; he was only around 16 at the time. We went up intermediate in 1982 and went through the whole year – league and championship – without losing a match.

That put us up to senior ranks for the first time ever as there were only the three grades at the time, and we stayed there for 16 or 17 years.

I was on the Cork senior panel for a lot of the 1980s, but I was nearly off the panel more than I was on it! I won an All-Ireland junior in 1983 – I was eligible as Milford were intermediate in '82. I was there or thereabouts always with the seniors but I couldn't get in – there was a very strong panel of players there at the time. Maybe I wasn't good enough, probably... or didn't believe enough in myself or whatever.

I had played a few league games and the Centenary Cup in 1984, but didn't make the panel for the Munster final that year. I made a championship appearance against Limerick in 1987 and I came on then in the Munster final replay against Tipp in Killarney. In 1989, things didn't happen for Cork. Tomás Mul and Kevin Hennessy weren't there… they had been left out, and Waterford beat us after a replay.

In the county championship that year, the Glen beat us by a point in Charleville and they went on and won the county. That's how Tomás was nominated as captain for 1990, after he was recalled, and the champions also had a selector, so that's how Liam Ó Tuama was chairman of the selection committee.

You'd Martin Coleman, Denis Hurley, Frank Murphy and the Canon. Gerald was trainer, but not a selector. The backroom then consisted of Tommy Lynch, who was looking after the gear, and you had 'Kid' Cronin and Frank Cogan as masseurs.

The Canon came back in and the first league match was against Galway in October 1989 in Páirc Uí Chaoimh – so the first game of the season was against them and, as things would turn out, the last one would be too.

That time, you mightn't even know you were on the panel until the week before the match… you'd see the paper on the Tuesday and then you'd receive a slip of paper in the post… *You have been selected…*

We beat Galway by two points, and 10 or 11 of the starting team that day were the same as would start the final the following September.

Unfortunately, Kieran Kingston, who also started that day, suffered a bad injury that would put him out for a lot of the year. Just before Christmas, we played a challenge match or some tournament game in Watergrasshill and the Canon was telling fellas to come back in some kind of shape in the new year.

We came back after Christmas and it was full steam ahead.

Gerald was in charge of the physical training and a lot of it centred around circuit training in the gym and running the tunnels in groups of four underneath the stands in Páirc Uí Chaoimh. When you pulled in there on a dark winter's night and you heard Tommy Lynch opening the big gates that separated each section, you knew it was going to be a tough one.

As the Canon used to say, there's no hiding place in the tunnels!

There were no shortcuts available. It was seen as a mental thing, really. One of the most important things was to pick your group – or at least know the fellas to avoid. Cathal Casey, Denis Walsh and those fellas were like rabbits, you couldn't touch them… you'd be looking for someone like Brendie O'Sullivan!

We were going well enough in the league, and I was playing at full-back and full-forward. I was No 14 for the semi-final against Wexford and Bryan Murphy from Bishopstown was full-back, but he got injured in the first-half of the drawn game and I ended up playing the rest of the game full-back.

The replay was in Nowlan Park on Easter Monday, and we had the same six forwards that would go on to start the All-Ireland final… and they only scored one point from play between them. The backs played well enough and I thought I did alright, but I'd say the Canon was scratching his head on the way home, wondering what was wrong.

The first game of the championship was against Kerry in Tralee and there were people wondering if we'd beat them. We won by nine points, but I pulled a hamstring after that and missed the Waterford game. Damien Irwin played left corner-back and I thought I'd be lucky to get back in, but I was chosen for the Munster final.

Prince played a gig in Páirc Uí Chaoimh in early July, so we were training in Ballinlough at the time and the Canon was playing backs and forwards every night above there. He roasted us; it was tough stuff, but there was a fabulous spirit being built up.

The Canon always respected your efforts and, once you gave of your best, he was happy. The main thing to avoid were those dreaded phone calls you might get from him at some hour of the night… and avoid being called in for 'confessions' at half-time in the match.

He always called out whether he had nine, 10, 11… or how many players were doing fine, so you were always left wondering… *Am I in the 10 or 11, or in the other four?*

Before the final, the view outside was that it would be a cake-walk for Tipp and we were under no pressure as we weren't being given a chance.

I used to travel to training with Pat Buckley and, after training, we used to stop for a 99 in O'Riordan's filling station in Blackpool. You needed something to help you cope with the old Mallow Road after a tough session!

I don't remember any talk about donkeys before the Munster final, and I don't think the Canon used it. Even though Tomás and Teddy were injured for the match, they played a huge role. The best memory I have is just before we went out on that field – there was a big circle inside in the dressing-room and the two of them stood inside in the middle of it and spoke to us.

If you could bottle that moment, you'd win every match.

We started well and then fell out of it a bit, but Mark Foley's goal just before half-time was huge and we finished well. It was a big win at the time, especially as nobody expected it. Kieran McGuckin captained us that day and did a great job.

We beat Antrim in the semi-final and then the build-up to the final against Galway was similar to the Tipp match in that we were the underdogs again. Pat Buckley was unlucky; he had played the semi-final but then he picked up an injury, and Teddy and Tomás were back, so he missed out on a starting spot for the final against Galway.

There was a very loyal core of lads that always came to Páirc Uí Chaoimh to watch us training and the backroom team were excellent. Frank Cogan had been through it himself, having won an All-Ireland football medal in 1973, and he always had a good ould word for you… very positive.

Then, the comment you'd get from the 'Kid' was, 'Jesus lads, I was sweating watching you!' Tommy Lynch would be in what was called 'the cave', where all the gear was, and the Canon would go in there before training and Tommy would have to tie his boots!

Then, there were nights when the Canon would take off… 'I don't need this!' We wouldn't be doing what he wanted, and he'd leave it to Gerald.

He was big into psychology.

It was all about getting the mind right. The other thing was that each fella had his own patch to win. Then the Canon had his car, a white Opel Vectra with the number plate 90-C-27 – the significance being that Cork were going for a 27th All-Ireland.

It was a sporty one and if you got a drive from the Canon, you'd know it!

Before we headed up to Dublin on the Saturday before the final, I met a friend of mine from Kilbrin – where I was primary school principal at the time – the late Denny Kearney. He said to me, 'Don't worry – you won't mind if you're held scoreless tomorrow!' I must say we got tremendous support from all of North Cork but especially from everyone in Milford and Kilbrin at the time.

We had actually played Galway twice in challenge matches in the run-up to the Munster final. The first one was a Sunday evening in Turloughmore, the day Ireland played Egypt in the World Cup. Bernie O'Connor was a Galway selector and he had a pub in Turloughmore, so we watched the soccer there before playing the game.

Then, at the start of July, we played them in Charleville on a Tuesday night. They beat us both times, but they were very competitive games.

I liked to get nervous on the Tuesday or Wednesday before the match and get rid of those nerves then. There were some days that it worked and some days that it didn't! I wouldn't think I was more nervous than usual just because it was my first senior final.

I think we were under less pressure if anything, nobody was giving us a chance. Dr Con Murphy and Kevin Hennessy kept things light anyway, there was always a good laugh… you weren't spared by them! *Just don't get caught in the crossfire…*

We were underdogs but we had a core of fellas who had won All-Irelands in 1984 and '86, including Tomás, who was a great captain. Nothing fazed him and he'd never flinch. Then, there was a link to the three in-a-row team as Gerald was playing and Martin Coleman was in goal, and Denis Hurley and Frank were both selectors.

Fellas used to go away and do their own thing on the Saturday night… it was fairly relaxed. However, I remember the morning of the match, I couldn't eat my breakfast. Frank Cogan said to force it down – at that time, we used to have a fry in the morning, if you can believe that!

We went to Na Fianna's grounds before going to Croke Park, just for a puck-around, and you could sense a tension among fellas – not necessarily nerves but anticipating a real tussle. Once I got to a stadium on the day of a big match, I always had to see the field.

Once I looked at the right-hand posts and the left-hand posts, it was a case of… *In between them now and that's it.*

I started on Michael McGrath, who was known as 'Hopper'. I was in full-back for a time, then myself and Denis switched, and I was on Noel Lane for a bit and Anthony Cunningham, who I knew reasonably well. The match went so fast.

It could have been over by half-time, but we survived it – Galway missed a few chances and we were still well in the match. Much was made of what was said at half-time but, to be honest, I don't remember.

We came out in the second-half, got some great scores – and Ger Cunningham's nose saved the day! – and we turned it around.

After coming back to The Burlington Hotel after the match, we were all shattered. I remember at one stage, I met Teddy, who was sitting at the top of the stairs. I sat down next to him and he said, 'I'm wrecked'.

I replied, 'Teddy, I don't know how you'll face it again in a fortnight's time?' and he said, 'It's just about getting through the next few hours!'

Pat Buckley and I came back to Milford late on the Monday night after the homecoming in Cork and it was great to see all the locals. I got into school on the Tuesday morning – not for very long – to a brilliant reception from both children and parents, and a half-day was granted immediately! There was a huge crowd there to congratulate me and the support from Milford and Kilbrin was excellent.

Funnily enough, Frank Murphy had predicted in his annual report for the county convention at the end of 1989 that there was a possibility of Cork winning a double, but I don't think many believed him.

Two weeks later, we all went to the football match together and we were there the Monday night after that, too. As a result, we got to know the footballers very well and that endured even to this day. Denis Conroy was chairperson at the time and he had the great quip that it had taken a century for Cork to win a double… but he did it in a fortnight!

I won an All Star that year and that had been the farthest thing from my mind – just winning the final was brilliant. There were six us – myself, Ger Cunningham, John Considine, Jim Cashman, Tony O'Sullivan and John Fitzgibbon.

I didn't do anything especially different that year, it was just the way things fell. I was just very lucky, really, more than anything else.

It's only like a blip now, when you think back. Whatever about the medals and the awards, it was the fun, the craic and the friendships that made it.

99

TOMÁS MULCAHY

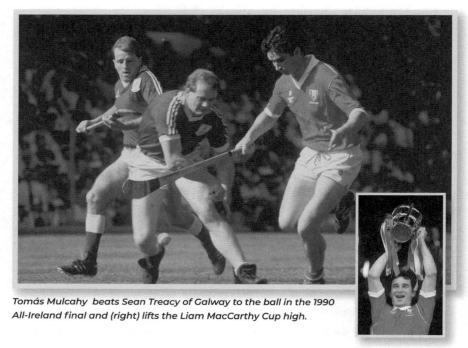

Tomás Mulcahy beats Sean Treacy of Galway to the ball in the 1990 All-Ireland final and (right) lifts the Liam MacCarthy Cup high.

"

MY LATE FATHER Gerald had an issue with his heart and he was told by his doctor – Dr Con Murphy – not to go to the final.

He went to a heart specialist in the Regional Hospital, Dr Fennell, and he said the same thing, to stay at home and watch it at home as it would be too dodgy. Of course, he went to the match and so, afterwards – after we had won – all that's on my mind is… *I hope he's okay?*

Back in the dressing-room, there was a great atmosphere.

The RTÉ cameras were there, getting a few interviews, and there's water flying everywhere and fellas clapping each other on the back and there's a sing-song.

Then, all of a sudden, the door burst open and who arrived in only my dad. Whatever way he did it, he had gone down to where the entrance to the dressing-rooms used to be, at the corner of the Hogan Stand and Canal End, and he had wangled his way in!

That made the occasion even further.

After Christmas 1989, we went back training properly and there was a group of us waiting outside Páirc Uí Chaoimh, for Tommy Lynch to open the gates and let us in.

We hear the screech of the brakes down the marina and this new car arrives, an Opel Vectra... you could see your face in the alloys, they were so shiny.

And who gets out, but himself. The boss man.

The Canon. 'Have a look at the registration plate,' he says.

90-C-27.

Fellas were wondering what's going on, until he explained. 'We've won 26 All-Ireland titles... and this year will be 27.'

I came on as a sub in the All-Ireland under-21 final against Galway in Birr in 1982. I was under-21 again in 1983 and I had a very good game against Waterford below in Páirc Uí Chaoimh. Johnny Clifford was senior manager at the time and I was asked if I wanted to join the panel.

There was a challenge match in Kinsale against Waterford on a Sunday night at 7pm. Here I am, walking into the dressing-room, and there were the likes of Jimmy Barry-Murphy, Tim Crowley, Seánie O'Leary, Johnny Crowley, Tom Cashman, John Fenton – they were the heroes that you were watching growing up, winning the three in-a-row.

I played that match and did well enough.

I came on against Limerick in the Munster Championship and kept my place after that, all the way up to the All-Ireland final, when Kilkenny beat us.

They say your first All-Ireland final can pass you by, before you realise what's going on, but I wouldn't say that was the case; I thought I did reasonably well. I was up against Dick O'Hara and he reminded me of Grizzly Adams, to be honest... strong and powerful, and a big, black beard coming out from under his helmet.

I got a goal and a point, but we lost and you always look back on the ones that got away. I think 1983 is one that we could have won.

We won in 1984 and '86 and I played in both, but at the start of '89 I was told by two selectors that I wasn't going to be part of the panel... 'Thanks for your time, you've done a wonderful job for Cork hurling, but we don't need to have you involved anymore'.

At the time, you were upset and hurt about it but, it's like in any sport, when a new management comes in they're entitled to make changes and pick who they want. Cork hurling had gone through a bad period after a dominant run of six or seven years.

Tipperary had taken over in Munster. I suppose fellas become a bit comfortable and maybe think they're guaranteed their place!

It was the biggest kick up the arse I ever got, to be honest, but I had to accept it and there were one or two others who were told the same.

That's the call that they made, but I drove on mad – as well as that, I had been captain of Glen Rovers in 1988 and we took a fair hammering in the county final against St Finbarr's. We had set our sights in Blackpool that this wasn't going to happen again. We had a very good team and we hadn't done ourselves justice.

We went back and put our shoulder to the wheel.

Donie O'Donovan, who had coached Cork to win the 1973 All-Ireland football title, was in charge and you had Glen stalwarts like John Lyons, Tom Corbett and Seánie Kennefick as selectors. I trained as hard as I could and we went and won the county, beating Sarsfields in the final.

To be fair to the selectors, Cork had played a couple of league games and they didn't go well, so they came back to me and asked me to re-join the panel, which I did, but I was injured for the championship match against Waterford – not that it's definite that I would have been picked.

I trained hard with the club and 1989 was a super year with Glen Rovers. I got a call from the Canon asking me to be part of his panel and, after that, I got the nomination from the club to be the captain.

The trends were set from a very early stage.

Gerald McCarthy – what a player he was, one of the best Cork produced in terms of striking ability – was coming in as the physical training coach, and also on the hurling side. A lot of the players would have worked with the Canon, either with Farranferris, UCC, Blackrock, the Cork minors in the 1970s or the seniors in 1984, so the pedigree was good.

There were a couple of harsh words among the players at the start of the year but, to be fair to the Canon, he set the bar big-time.

The Canon had a go at fellas, but he knew the fellas he could have a go at.

He kept saying to us, 'I've been with a good few of ye before and my job is to get back out of ye what I got out of ye in the past'.

The league semi-final against Wexford that we played up in Nowlan Park was an absolute disaster. We got one point from play. They say we don't like the cold weather or the rain, and that was never more epitomised than that day. The hailstones that came down were nearly as big as the sliothar.

Fellas – including myself – were nearly hiding behind the corner-backs and wing-backs... *Here boy, if you want the ball, here you go.* Fellas were shouting back to Cunningham, 'Don't be pucking it down on top of me, I don't want it at all'

After that, we got an unbelievable slating in the press.

The Cork Examiner and *Evening Echo* tore us asunder, but when you're backed into a corner, there's often a reaction and there was something that came out of it on that basis there was a bit of hurt there.

We'll show them!!

That's what transpired Nobody gave us a chance in the Munster final but the Canon had that belief in the team. Our training was hard, but very much in the style of the old Cork hurling – keep the ball going, no catching in the air... if you're centre-forward then your job is to get it to the inside line.

The Canon kept reiterating how you had to be in under your man, you couldn't be standing off him. If you don't connect and he doesn't catch, the ball goes through.

There was great spirit there.

I got injured about three weeks before the Munster final.

We played Cork under-21s in a challenge match on a Monday night and I went out to collect a ball, there was a pull across and it went right up my hurley and split my finger.

I knew straightaway I was in trouble; the finger was facing the sky.

Dr Con was there and he sent me straight to the Regional Hospital. It was badly broken in a couple of places. I was in hospital there for three or four days and they thought they might be able to put it back in place and that it would heal itself, but that wasn't happening and so I had to get it pinned.

The doctor was from Pakistan and I was trying to explain to him about hurling and the Munster final, but he wasn't having any of it!

'No, no, no, you won't play any game!' he said, but I never gave up hope.

On the day before the game, I went out to Dr Con's house for a fitness test in his back garden. He had a hurley and I had a hurley, and he told me to pull against him in the air – as soon as I did, I had to drop the hurley out of my hand, the pain was too much.

Kieran McGuckin was captain that day and it was a famous victory. In the dressing-room beforehand, you could sense that that team wasn't going to be beaten. The drive, the adrenaline, the spirit, the camaraderie, the focus… it was all because we were totally written off.

We were complete underdogs in everybody's eyes. Tipperary had won the All-Ireland in 1989 and they were raging favourites to win it again.

Cork sensed their chance and that was crucial.

Everyone prepares differently for a matchday, often they're in their own bubbles. Some guys are hitting a ball off the wall, some are inside in the toilets, some are marching up and down… and some are sitting with their head in between their knees, not saying a word. This time, there was something different – everybody was buzzed, everybody was hyped.

When Teddy and I spoke to the team, we knew that they would actually have broken the doors to get out, they were that fired.

There were some unbelievable displays that day – Mark Foley stole the day, obviously, and I'm sure it's one he'll remember for a long, *long* time but it was the team performance that was the big thing. The collective spirit there that day was just incredible and that goes down to the Canon and to Gerald.

I came back and captained the team for the All-Ireland semi-final against Antrim; I started corner-forward and went out centre-forward. It was a very tough match and, maybe, after the high of the Munster final, we took them a little bit for granted.

It was one that we got over and we let the other semi-final take care of itself. On the way back down on the train, we were hearing that Galway had beaten Offaly… so it was Cork-Galway again. We hadn't shot the lights out against Antrim, and Galway were very impressive against Offaly, so they were strong favourites.

They had a lost a few in the 1980s that they felt they should have won, 1986 in particular, and the Canon and Gerald were quick to drum it into us that Galway had never beaten Cork in a hurling final.

By this stage, you could have a couple of hundred at our training sessions and, after the last one on the Wednesday night, the crowd got up to give us a standing ovation. There was a sense that there was a bit of belief coming back to the Cork public that this could be our year.

Wednesday was light – a bit of a jog, puck a few balls and maybe do a few interviews and then out the gap.

You put the hurley away and didn't see it again until the weekend.

We travelled on the Saturday, the 1.40pm train.

In the morning, you're getting up at home and getting ready, getting your gear and before you know it. you're heading to the station. You're going back into the company of the guys you've been with for the last couple of years and it's fantastic.

The craic on those trains used to be incredible. You had characters on the team and among the management – for instance, Frank Murphy wasn't shy when it came around to giving a slag to anyone.

Dr Con was called the sixth selector, and he was part and parcel of it.

If a fella had had a write-up that morning in the *Examiner*, or the *Echo* the night before, you were taken to pieces but it was all in good spirits. The main man for us in terms of the banter was Kevin Hennessy – what a character. Absolutely nothing was safe with Kevin; if you told him something and made him promise not to tell anyone, you were guaranteed that everyone would know within a few minutes!

That was all part of the team ethos – it wasn't about individuals or clubs, it was all about Cork.

You get to the hotel and have a bit of grub and by this stage there are huge crowds around, because everyone knows that when Cork go to Dublin they stay at The Burlington Hotel! The place would be packed and so you're better off going somewhere else – some lads would go to the pictures or go for a walk, but I used to go to Shelbourne Park, following the tradition Jimmy Barry-Murphy had started. He trained us well!

Fellas might have had £2 or a fiver on a dog but it passed away the night. Then – hard to believe now – we might have a pint or two on the way back.

Back for 10.15pm and a team meeting.

A pint of milk and a sandwich, and off to bed.

I was rooming with Kevin and he was working in Kepak in Watergrasshill at the time – he used to start his shift at 5.30am and All-Ireland final weekend was no different. He was up early, showering, pulling the curtains back.

'Look at the beautiful morning outside!' to which the response was, 'Kevin, if you don't close those curtains, I'll throw you out the window!'

Then he's fidgety, reading papers, waiting until he can go down to have his breakfast. He goes down by himself and comes back up, hitting a ball off the wall with his hurley – no regard for the fellas in the next room who are trying to sleep!

That was Kevin and that was his way: other fellas might stay in bed until 10am or others would go for a walk or a puck-around. There are incredible memories when you look back at what went on – would they happen now?

Probably not.

All-Ireland final day is a big thing, to be walking around in the parade behind the Artane Boys Band and seeing people in the crowd and so on – it's a massive, *massive* occasion and it by-passes some guys.

The build-up is two or three weeks and then, in 70 minutes, *it's gone* and you can't go back and change it.

We had some harsh words at half-time.

We started very well and then missed a few bad frees. On the other side, Galway missed a pile as well and probably felt that they could have been ahead by more than five points. In the dressing-room, we were saying that we hadn't played at all… and we were still well in the game – in hurling, five points is *nothing*.

It was always drilled into us not to let the heads drop, that a lead can be overturned.

I think the beauty for us as a team, even back to 1984 and '86, was that, when a goal was on, we gave the ball to the guy in the best position. It didn't matter who got the goals and there was a great spread that day.

We used to always be slagging Tony O'Sullivan… 'When are you going to join in, when are you going to get a goal like the other five?!' – but, of course, Tony would score six or seven points!

It was something that we practised in training.

The Canon would throw out 10 or 15 balls and you're taking on Ger Cunningham, trying to make him work. The Canon and Gerald loved to see goals scored and the amount we got in that period was just incredible.

On the Sunday morning, seven or eight of us went for a walk near the Burlington. My Glen clubmate John Fitzgibbon was in the group and he had a deep love of Christy Ring – he could tell you anything about him. He could go through all the matches Ring played and what he had scored; how he'd hit the ball off his left and right; who his toughest opponents were and so on.

Dr Con asked John how he'd celebrate if he scored a goal that day.

Off John went up the footpath, five or six feet ahead of us, two hands in the air.

'I'm going to celebrate like Ringy!' he said. Ten minutes into the second-half, Ger Fitzgerald went down injured and Dr Con had to treat him. As he was leaving Ger to go back around the pitch, he went into John.

'What was all that talk about the celebration this morning? The boys are talking about you over on the line, isn't it about time you did something?'

By the time he had got to the dugout, Fitzy had scored two goals!

That was John – he could be starved of possession for a long time but all he needed was one or two chances, and he'd bury them. Of course, Dr Con took the credit – the selectors weren't talking about John at all, but he felt that he needed a jolt.

The public were enthralled with that match.

It was free-scoring, up and down the field. We got five goals, they got two, so seven in all. To be part of a game like that and to come out on the right side of it was incredible, all the more so to be captain of the team.

To follow in the footsteps of great names like Jack Lynch, Connie Buckley, Christy Ring, Martin O'Doherty in being a winning Cork captain from the Glen was a really proud thing. Kieran McGuckin and John Fitzgibbon were joining the band of winners too and I'm sure the other guys on the team felt the same in terms of their own clubs.

When you go up the Hogan Stand, it's unbelievable… you're being pulled and dragged, clapped on the back, fellas are trying to pull the hurley out of your hand!

When I look back at it now, I'm there with the President of the GAA and two seats behind is my hero, Jack Lynch. Maybe I should have brought him down to lift the cup with me… it would have been a nice memory.

As a player, I wouldn't have seen him play but, what I heard about him and then, having met him on a few occasions, he was so impressive. When we won the county in 1989, he was there on Christy Ring Bridge when we arrived with the cup.

The man oozed charisma and there he was, two rows back.

It's grand being captain and accepting the cup, but it is all about the team. We were at the function on the Sunday night and I won Man of the Match, but I don't think I deserved to get it. We were sitting at the table and Seán O'Gorman and Jim Cashman were there too.

As Michael Lyster was about to announce the winner, I moved my seat because I thought it would be Seán going up. Then my name was called out and I was a bit dumb-struck, wondering where that had come from.

Maybe the goal was important and I did well after moving from corner-forward to centre-forward, but everybody was brilliant.

I accepted it, but everybody was Man of the Match.

Two weeks afterwards, the footballers winning Sam Maguire was the icing on the cake. You're part of history then and you're wondering if it'll ever be repeated again.

It's long time ago and maybe people think we're making too much of 1990, but it's still a very strong memory for me.

It's sad to think it was so long ago, though… it only feels like yesterday!

DENIS WALSH

CORK 2-12 TIPPERARY 1-12
Munster SHC Semi-Final
Páirc Uí Chaoimh
JUNE 7, 1992

Victory over Tipperary in the titanic Munster semi-final clash in 1992 allowed Cork to progress to the provincial final where (above) Denis Walsh tussles with Limerick's Gary Kirby.

★ **CORK:** G Cunningham; S O'Gorman, D Mulcahy, B Corcoran (0-2); C Casey, J Cashman, **D Walsh**; T McCarthy, S McCarthy; T Kelleher, T Mulcahy (1-0), T O'Sullivan (0-7); G Fitzgerald (0-1), K Hennessy (0-1), J Fitzgibbon (1-1). Subs: P Buckley for Kelleher, P Hartnett for S McCarthy.

★ **TIPPERARY:** K Hogan; P Delaney, N Sheehy, G Frend; Colm Bonnar, B Ryan, Conal Bonnar; D Carr (0-1), A Ryan (0-2); M Cleary (0-3), D Ryan (1-1), J Leahy; P Fox (0-2), Cormac Bonnar, N English. Subs: C Stakelum (0-3) for Cormac Bonnar, R Ryan for Colm Bonnar.

THE ACTION

AS IN 1990, Tipperary's reign as All-Ireland champions was brought to an end by Cork, albeit in a game that was more of a dour battle than the Munster final in Thurles two years previously.

The year before, the sides had drawn at Páirc Uí Chaoimh before Tipp triumphed in a replay to dethrone Cork. They had not won against Cork in Cork since a 1922 triumph at what was then the Athletic Grounds and, with a slight wind behind them in the first-half, Tipp had the game's opening two points courtesy of Michael Cleary frees – while it took until the 15th minute before Tony O'Sullivan got Cork off the mark.

Overall, both sets of backs were on top in that opening half and there were no goal chances of any real quality. With Cathal Casey and Teddy McCarthy beginning to gain supremacy, Cork's challenge was in the ascendancy as they went in trailing at half-time but just a point, 0-6 to 0-5.

Less than a minute into the second-half, teenage corner-back Brian Corcoran – enjoying a debut season that would see him win Hurler of The Year – levelled with a free from well inside his own half, before Tony O'Sullivan put them ahead for the first time. Then the game was fully turned on its head thanks to a John Fitzgibbon goal, after Kevin Hennessy broke down a Casey delivery. When influential substitute Pat Buckley won a free, O'Sullivan converted to put Cork five clear.

By this stage, the Cork defence had all but shut down the Tipp threat and Kevin Hennessy could have added a second goal, hooking the ball over the bar from close range. In the wake of that, Tipp had two scores from Conor Stakelum dead balls but Tomás Mulcahy's goal, touching home a Casey sideline cut, put Cork eight clear.

That lead had been reduced to six when Declan Ryan did get a Tipperary goal in the second minute of injury-time, but there was no time for a late equaliser to materialise.

Cork would go on to see off Limerick in the Munster final but, after an All-Ireland semi-final win over Down, Kilkenny would get the better of them in the decider that September.

★★★★★

66

I'D BE VERY much into the psychology of the whole sport. When you come up against an opponent, it might have nothing to do with ability or skill or anything like that... you could be winning a battle or getting something over a guy, for other reasons.

If you look at 1992, and the Cork and Tipperary teams that day... they were probably at their most experienced. There were only two players, one on each team, who were inexperienced – George Frend played corner-back for Tipp, and Timmy Kelleher played wing-forward for us. Nearly every other player had two All-Ireland medals in the back pocket. We had all been there since 1986, give or take, and there was a perception at the time that the famine was over... that Tipp were back and they had it over Cork.

But if you looked at the whole thing, that wasn't necessarily the case.

They had beaten us in a replay in 1987. They beat us fair and square in 1988, when we were kind of in disarray. We didn't play them in 1989 and they won the All-Ireland. And then we beat them in that famous game in 1990, obviously. We won the All-Ireland and then they came along in 1991 and beat us after a replay, and went on to win the All-Ireland, again.

Subconsciously, all of the Cork players knew that, if they beat us again, in 1992, over that period it would have been 4-1 to Tipperary. We beat them and it was probably one of the most physical games that I was ever involved in. The hits came thick and fast, and the ferocity was unreal, though it did probably die off a bit in the second-half. Twenty-five minutes into that match, it was 0-4 to 0-2, which probably tells you everything you need to know.

I picked a team a while back of the greatest players I ever played against and there were four Tipp forwards on it – John Leahy, Declan Ryan, Pat Fox and Nicholas English. They all played that day, but we confined them to six points in the first-half and six points in the second-half. Denis Mulcahy was brought back... it was his first game back for two years, and he did a job on Cormac Bonnar.

Tipp got a goal with the last puck of the game, so it finished 2-12 to 1-12.

There were a lot of hits, a lot of afters and nobody blinked. When you think of the space that opens up in today's game, it was in contrast to that day when there wasn't much room at all in which to manoeuvre. We had decided a few days beforehand that the game would be played on our terms and not theirs, and I'm afraid we had to be strong to tell our own management that as well, to be honest!

In both 1987 and '91, we were All-Ireland champions and they had beaten us. This was our chance to stake our claim. It was savage. Just look at the first 20 minutes of that match and the hits, with fellas diving into tackles – in today's game, there'd probably be about six gone! We threw everything at them in the first-half and we got a goal and a point just after half-time to go five points clear. The game kind of fizzled out after that.

To me, it was a significant game because it actually spelled the end for both teams, really. We were flat for the rest of the year – we were flat against Limerick for the Munster final, which we won, and then flat in the All-Ireland final as well.

That's not belittling Kilkenny's achievement – they won the final fair and square, with DJ Carey playing so well. We had every opportunity to make a good impact but, even in the Munster final against Limerick – when Tomás Mul got the infamous goal where he switched the ball from one hand to the other – we were in trouble and just got over the line.

We were finished as a team after that and, as it turned out, so were Tipp. They won Munster the following year, but Galway beat them in the All-Ireland semi-final.

I played at No. 7 that day.

I played there in the 1986 All-Ireland final and I was full-back for the '90 final – in fact, I started championship games for Cork in every one of the six back positions. Any fella would have a favoured slot. It was probably centre-back for me, but I don't think I was athletic enough to play there at inter-county level.

No 4 or 7 was probably where I was most comfortable, but I often played at 2 or 5. I suppose I was a man-marker in a lot of cases.

That day, I was on Michael Cleary, who tried to run the hell out of me but I'd say he ran the hell out of himself, as it turned out!

Thirty years ago, there wasn't as much opposition analysis or anything like that, but I was always a very deep thinker about players I'd be facing... whether they turned left or right... or which side they'd shoot from. If I saw my colleague at right corner-back, say, on a fella that I had often marked, I'd say to him, 'Look, that guy always turns left, so if he throws a dummy to the right you know he'll come back'.

There was no video analysis but we'd have discussions ourselves. Ultimately, though, you were left to your own devices and it was sink or swim.

We brought in Pat Buckley and Pat Hartnett from the bench, so even if guys weren't performing, you had a serious calibre of player to come in, as well. Almost all of those players knew one another like the back of their hands. George Frend played left corner-back for Tipp and he was only 22, but he had a great game. Timmy Kelleher was right half-forward for us and he was taken off at half-time – he was a right half-back rather than a forward, but I could see what we were trying to do.

Another thing that made it special was that the two St Catherine's players were the wing-backs, either side of Jim Cashman. Cathal Casey played a great game that day, so it was a highlight for the club.

Cathal was two years younger than me but he had been on the bench in 1986, when he was only 19. Prior to that, John Murphy, who passed away recently, had been a minor in 1975 when Cork lost the All-Ireland final and Christy Clancy was a minor in '82. Donal O'Leary and Shane O'Connell would have played under-21 for Cork in the mid-to-late 80s, and then Kieran Morrison and Johnny Sheehan were minor and under-21 in the 90s and on the senior panel in 1999.

I went to a football college, Coláiste an Chroí Naofa in Carraig na bhFear. There was no hurling there really prior to us going there, but then there were a few of us from East Cork and lads from North Cork. We got going, but we were still only C or B grade, never Harty.

There's no doubt that the breakthrough for me was St Catherine's becoming prominent.

We reached the 1981 junior final… Milford beat us, and I played as an under-16… it wouldn't be allowed nowadays! When we came back two years later to win the junior, I was playing centre-forward.

Even though I was still a minor, I was nearly a veteran at that stage. That helped me to get noticed. If I was able to hold my own as a teenager in what was still the third tier, the selectors were probably saying I was worth a look.

By 1992, I was only playing hurling but, in terms of whether it improved me, I don't think I would have noticed that. Certain commentators were always saying it, but that's only narrative. I loved changing over from one to the other, from hurling to football, and back, to be honest. Once you stayed injury-free, it was a breath of fresh air to switch over and back.

The modern-day player will talk about dedicating his life to it so many nights of the week and you might wonder what we were doing, but we were doing exactly the same. We mightn't be down the field or in the gym every night of the week, but the chances are that fellas were doing stuff that you mightn't know about, or they mightn't have been publicising it.

I had played minor hurling for two years and in the second of those seasons I was on the under-21 panel too... so I played under-21 for four years. Teddy Mac was the same age and he was under-21 for four years too – interestingly enough, we never qualified for a Munster final in any of those six campaigns.

You hear the talk today that you must be winning this or that at underage to be successful at senior, but we didn't even make a final!

I was brought along a bit on the senior panel. I remember playing at the opening of a pitch above in Spiddal in 1984, when I was still only 19, and I was even brought to a behind-closed-doors game a few weeks before that year's All-Ireland final in Thurles. Seánie O'Leary, who only passed away recently, was on the bench with me.

I got a few games. I even played centre-forward in a league game against Galway in 1985, before I moved back down the field. Having watched from the bench, I was well tuned-in by the time my turn came around to play championship.

But it was still massive.

I was playing alongside guys that had been on the three in-a-row team – Johnny Crowley, Dermot McCurtain, Tom Cashman, John Fenton. It was unreal stuff.

You'd have to pinch yourself.

Before I picked up a hurley, I was watching these guys! They were brilliant. Johnny Crowley was a hero of mine and, next thing, I'm playing alongside him. That was fascinating and a great learning curve.

They were great guys to learn from and there was no bullshit with them.

The Canon was a larger-than-life figure. He could come up with anything, really, but on the training ground Gerald was the man for the basic stuff and the nitty-gritty. He was such an amazing player himself. I had been watching him over the years; he was a guy from whom you were going to soak up the info. That was brilliant, to have that experience on the line, and between the two of them there was a good balance there.

It was a fantastic year in 1990, though there was a major disappointment for me at the end of the year when I didn't get the two All-Ireland medals, even though I had played in the two Munster finals. That's bureaucracy for you!

When you look back on it, it was amazing, but at the time it was just tunnel-vision, really, going from one game to the next. You didn't even think negatively about what it might have been like to lose two finals – and that could easily have happened, we were underdogs against Galway and Meath.

From that point of view, it makes it even more of an achievement – don't forget that we won the game against Meath with 14 men for most of the game.

It's often said that Páirc Uí Chaoimh wasn't as good as Thurles for a big game but, that day, there must have been 45,000 in the Páirc… full to the rafters. That was special, and obviously Thurles was too, but that had as much to with tradition and the chances were that you were always going to get a crowd in Semple Stadium.

Before a match in the Páirc, we often went down to Blackrock for a puck-around, but there wasn't a big pre-match thing of getting together three hours beforehand or anything like that. You'd get there about an hour and a half ahead of the game, and that might vary depending on who was in charge, or the size of the occasion or whatever.

I had a few quirky things.

I always liked to be last out of the dressing-room and if there was a photograph to be taken, I liked to be on the left hand side of the back row… the right as you'd look at it. You mightn't always get your choice, though!

I never really wore a helmet – I tried one for a month or so but it didn't work, I felt like a jack-in-the-box and I had to discard it again! However, I always wore a gumshield and I always wore shin-guards. My teeth were a bit rigid and every time I got a touch on the lip it would split wide open.

I often played matches with stitches in my lips; you were hardly going to be telling Gerald or the Canon that couldn't play because of a cut in the mouth!

The shin-guards?

I suppose I got such a doing at a young age from fellas pulling on the ground that my shins were destroyed. I'd no choice with either of them.

From a point of view of looking at it psychologically, all great sport is based on rivalry. We had that rivalry with Tipp and we had to make our case that day.

If you look at the current Limerick team – which I'm a great fan of, they're unbelievable – they've won three All-Irelands in four years and they were unlucky to lose to Kilkenny in 2019, so they could be going for five in-a-row, but where is their rivalry?

The closest thing to a rival they have is Waterford and they've beaten them in their games. They've hammered Cork. You could argue that it's Tipp, but they dismantled them last year even with a 10-point head-start.

Obviously, they've a bee in their bonnet over Kilkenny but it's not a back-and-forth.

In 1992, it was a case of Ali vs Frazier… seconds out!

We knew that it would be a heavyweight affair and the loser was going to be out. That's the beauty of the knockout system, a sense of… *This is it…do or die!*

And there's something special about that.

I'm not saying that we were a better team than Tipperary. We beat them twice, they beat us three times, but in two of those they needed a replay. Let's be honest, there wasn't much between the teams. That Tipp team could easily have won three, four… five in-a-row. They won in 1989 and felt that '90 was there for the taking.

They won again in 1991 and if they had beaten us in '92 then they might well have gone on and beaten Kilkenny, like the previous year.

We felt that the tide was turning in Tipperary's favour in relation to dominance over Cork. Whatever about winning Munsters or All-Irelands, we felt – without there being any animosity there – that that was a day where we had to win at all costs.

99

SEÁNIE McGRATH

CORK 0-23 TIPPERARY 3-12
Munster SHC Final
Semple Stadium
JULY 2, 2000

Seánie McGrath is carried off the field in Thurles, after Cork's victory over arch rivals Tipperary in 2000.

★ **CORK:** D Óg Cusack; F Ryan, D O'Sullivan, J Browne; W Sherlock, B Corcoran, S Óg Ó hAilpín; D Barrett (0-1), M O'Connell; T McCarthy, F McCormack, A Browne (0-3); **S McGrath (0-3)**, J Deane (0-10), B O'Connor (0-3). Subs: P Ryan (0-2) for O'Connell, K Murray (0-1) for McCormack.

★ **TIPPERARY:** B Cummins; P Ormonde, P Maher, Michael Ryan; J Carroll, D Kennedy, E Corcoran; J Leahy (0-1), T Dunne (2-0); M O'Leary, E Enright (0-2), B O'Meara (0-2); E O'Neill (1-5), P Shelley, P O'Brien. Subs: L Cahill (0-1) for O'Brien, Micheál Ryan for O'Leary, P Kelly (0-1) for Shelley.

THE ACTION

CORK WERE AIMING to win back-to-back Munster titles for the first time since 1986, with wins over Kerry and Limerick sending the reigning All-Ireland champions through to a first championship meeting with Tipperary since 1992.

A truly absorbing contest was to ensue in Thurles.

Cork had only conceded one goal in four matches en route to winning the All-Ireland title in 1999, but they were to concede three here, as well as needing to repel two Tipperary penalties. The first of those was awarded in the 11th minute as Paul Shelley was hauled down by Cork goalkeeper Dónal Óg Cusack, but Diarmuid O'Sullivan blocked Tommy Dunne's shot.

After that let-off, Cork edged matters, Seán Óg Ó hAilpín showing up strongly for them, while Joe Deane was in superb form in attack.

They were 0-6 to 0-5 in front when Eugene O'Neill netted for Tipp – seeking their first Munster title since 1993 – but Jimmy Barry-Murphy's team were level by half-time.

Ben O'Connor put Cork ahead again on the restart and, though Tipp replied with three straight points, the introduction of Pat Ryan at midfield helped Cork to gain a foothold as they moved 0-16 to 1-10 ahead.

While Tipp were level through a marvellous Dunne goal, Cork's composure couldn't be shaken – they had four points in the space of six minutes that also included a second Tipp penalty – John Leahy's effort repelled on this occasion.

A second Dunne goal ensured that Tipp were never out of touch, but Cork's point-scoring capacity was such that they always stayed far enough ahead.

★★★★★

66

GROWING UP IN the 1980s, our household was as much about a Cork-Tipp Munster final, as it was about an All-Ireland final.

Cork in the 80s were obviously competing regularly in All-Ireland finals, but the day out going up to Thurles was always about a Cork-Tipp Munster final, with respect to Limerick, Waterford and Clare.

We beat Clare in my first Munster final in 1999 and we *had* to get over them as they had beaten us in '97 and '98, but to play in a provincial decider against Tipp was special.

The build-up to it!

There were two great managers, who had such brilliant Munster final records – Nicky English with Tipp, and obviously Jimmy with ourselves – that it added to it. There was just such a sense of occasion for me, as a personal dream of mine was always to play in a Cork-Tipp Munster final… and especially for it to be in Thurles.

The game itself, the occasion, the result, the way we won it… it all just typified what I had been reared on in hurling terms.

For me, it was as much about the history of the fixture.

The Tony Forristal Tournament at under-14 level was the first real opportunity to stamp your mark at inter-county – if you want to call it that, even though we were only kids, really – but I failed to make that panel. I made an under-16 selection, but that was a city divisional team for a Munster regional competition.

John Meyler was in charge of us and we won it – the final was against a Tipperary selection, it might have been Mid-Tipp, and it was played the day of the 1991 Munster final in Páirc Uí Chaoimh at 12 noon, before the minor game.

That was the first taste of it, even though it was only played in front of a hundred or so people there at that hour of the day. For the senior match, we were allowed to sit behind the City End goal – we were nearly able to throw our hand up and catch the players, they were that close to us.

For me growing up, it was about the playing and the training and the skills, but also about seeing your heroes and trying to mimic them. That day in 1991, it was an incredible atmosphere, albeit kind of a wet day.

The 2000 final was quite the opposite… early July and very warm, and it had all of the ingredients that you'd expect from a Cork-Tipp Munster final.

I had played minor in 1992 and '93 and we lost to Tipp both years.

In 1992, John Meyler was the manager and we lost to them in the first round. Then, the following year, Jimmy was manager and they beat us in the Munster final inside in Limerick.

Jimmy was heavily involved in the club scene as well and, at that time, the Barrs were the dominant team at minor and under-21.

We would have played them regularly – it was all about trying to win the city division and get out into the county, so they were our real nemesis. From 1991 to '93, they beat us in two city finals and a semi-final, and Jimmy was manager of those teams.

He was on a different level completely as a player, but you try to take nuggets from them all. He was a goal-getter and one of the greats – I was small so it was just a case that my game was to be in the square and try to win a bit of ball, focusing on first touch and things like that.

I had some great coaches with the Glen, too.

The club have had some fantastic players, but coming up along, the guys that coached us mightn't have been huge names. The first introduction to hurling I had in the Glen was with Paul McCarthy, who was great at underage. He didn't have a huge playing career but he was an incredible tutor and mentor.

Liam Cashman of Cashmans' Bookmakers used to look after our underage teams and Micheál Kelleher was another guy there – they all fostered a love of the game and a love of the jersey, and worked tirelessly on our skills. They were all incredible volunteers and they adored the club and really got a great kick out of developing players to go on and play at whatever grade.

Whether it was senior, intermediate or junior, they didn't care once they got fellas participating beyond minor and into adult hurling.

I know it meant a lot to people to see me progress.

Before the All-Ireland in 1999, Richie Kelleher organised a bit of a get-together up in the club on the Friday night and the lads had a few novelty items saying, 'Well done' and 'Best of luck' – though some of them weren't exactly clean for print!

They were unbelievable supporters and friends, and they'd be the first gang you'd meet after a game – Kevin Fox, Kenny 'Cal', Liam Galvin… all those fellas. They were all buddies that I played with underage, coming all the way up… Richie included, and it was special for them, as much as it was for me.

In 1997, I was called up to the Cork panel.

I had made my Glen debut when I was 17 – I came on as a sub in the 1993 championship. The team was strong, with some household names.

There John and Kieran Fitzgibbon, Ger O'Riordan, Tomás Mulcahy, Liam Martin… the older Pat Horgan was still there. Johnny Clifford was the manager and it was the be-all and the end-all at the time to playing alongside them.

Back then, it was straight knockout and Na Piarsaigh beat us in the first round. We used to go to the Sunset Ridge for a bit of grub after training on the Thursday night – and Johnny's speech to the lads and his instructions… I'd never experienced anything like that. He was such a God around the club and it was just incredible to be witnessing it and to be part of it, hearing such a great man give an oration like that.

It was a great time to be a young player in Cork as there was a lot of rebuilding going on. The team had struggled to make any real impression in the championship from 1993 to '96. I had a good club campaign in 1996; we got to the semi-final and were beaten by Avondhu in a replay.

I scored well that year and I captained the under-21s to win Munster.

I was enjoying my hurling at the time, so I felt that I had a right chance. I was in UCC but I hadn't played Fitzgibbon up to then – Dr Paddy Crowley got on to me in the winter of 1996 to get involved and I did. I came to love that competition.

I went on to have two enjoyable years in it, in 1997 and '98. We won it against Garda College in 1997 and I did well, so I had a feeling that I was definitely in the mix, especially as Cork were looking for new talent and a bit of a shake-up.

All of those factors gave me a great opportunity – I was obviously overjoyed and honoured, but I did feel I had a chance of a call-up.

It probably sounds a bit clichéd, but it really was a case of taking it one game at a time with Cork. After such a long time without success, Cork's focus was on trying to win championship games – there was no talk of winning All-Irelands.

When we beat Limerick in 1998, that was Cork's first win over anyone apart from Kerry since '92. When you talk about rebuilding a team, there was ferocious change – that was the quintessential example.

Winning the league in 1998 was huge for the team and Jimmy put huge stock in that. He wanted us to get that feeling of what winning was about. We were beaten by Clare in the 1998 championship – people said we were hockeyed, it finished 0-21 to 0-13 – but we were competitive for 50-odd minutes and only tailed away with a bit of inexperience at the end.

Going into 1999, Jimmy built up an incredible morale in the camp and winning the All-Ireland was amazing. Ultimately, we failed to match that in 2000 – we lost to Offaly in the All-Ireland semi-final – but the focus initially was to try to go back-to-back in Munster championships.

We beat Kerry fairly easily in the first game and then I got a goal in the semi-final win over Limerick. Later on, when I got involved in management myself, I could see how challenging it was to keep a team's morale going.

It's what makes you realise what an achievement it was for Kilkenny in the 2000s to win four in-a-row. The thing for Jimmy in 2000 was to keep the morale going and keep the appetite going, and ensure fellas didn't wane in their hunger. That's another reason why winning Munster that year was such a thrill, backing up the previous year.

Getting over the line against Tipp, the way we did, showed that we weren't just a one-off.

When you're light, people might assume that you're fit and you don't get tired and all that, but I was always very conscious of my fitness.

You know your own body and I'd make sure that, two weeks out from a game, I'd train extremely hard so I'd know I was in the right shape – and then taper off in the week of the match.

Every player will tell you that touch is important but, especially when I had no real physicality to go with my game, I had to make sure it was razor-sharp.

I wasn't going to win too many second balls, so I had to make sure I was going to win the first one! Coming up to championship, I used to be out the back constantly, hitting off the wall – and, as I got older, that was probably where I found that I was struggling a bit, as I wasn't able to put that time into it with work and everything else that was going on.

When you're young, care-free and single and things are going handy, that was a big thing for me – thousands of balls off the wall, outside of training.

It wasn't just the Tuesday and Thursday nights, it was every night of the week, just making sure that touch was there.

On the panel, you'd forge relationships.

Diarmuid O'Sullivan was a great pal of mine and Seánie O'Farrell too, so you'd invariably end up sitting next to one of them on the bus.

You'd have a bit of craic and I was probably classed as a bit of a joker in the pack, but I still knew that, come championship day, you had to get your timing right. You might have a laugh going on but, certainly, once you hit Dundrum and going from there to Thurles, it was definitely a case of getting the game-face on.

I was an easy-enough-going, jovial kind of character anyway, I wasn't putting on any front, but I used to feel nervous, too. I think a fella is lying if he says that he goes through a championship game – especially of that magnitude – care-free, breezy and with no nerves.

Looking back, you'd kind of miss those nerves!

They were great nerves, it's hard to describe them, almost a culmination of everything in your career coming through 70 minutes of hurling.

I loved that feeling, to be honest.

One change in terms of appearance that I made for 2000 was to start wearing my socks up. Growing up, I was a fan of John Fitzgibbon and he used to always do that, so I said I'd have a rattle off it but I don't know how stupid I looked with the skinny legs! He was an idol and it was an opportunity to mimic him.

The Tipp match was a funny game, because we didn't hurl terribly well but were hanging in there. Pat Ryan came on and had a great game.

I don't think Tipp were ever rolling over us but they got incredible goals – I think it's fair to say that the two goals Tommy Dunne got were among the best ever scored in a Munster final. They were sensational.

It's weird, because you're in the middle of a game and you should be focusing on your own task and all of that but I remember, especially for the second goal, thinking… *Wow!*

I started on Michael Ryan and then, half-way through the second-half, I was moved out wing-forward and I ended up on John Carroll. I got three points, but I do remember missing one just before the end!

It was the kind of a wide that used to annoy Jimmy, so I was thinking that I'd better get another chance as he would have been livid. After that miss, Paul Kelly got a point for Tipp to bring it back to a point and I was feeling like I had made a bit of a mess of it but, luckily, I got another chance and it went over.

After a game like that – and even during it, though you're trying your best to stay focused – you think about your parents and your uncles and so on.

All of my family would be massively steeped in the game and anybody who plays to a high level would say that all of those people are ringing you prior to the game or they're getting the bus up to support you... or they're meeting you in the pub after.

Meeting those people in Liberty Square in Thurles afterwards, you feel like you've achieved for them as well, because Cork hurling meant so much to them. The whole family combination that goes with it makes it so much more special.

We would have loved to have had another crack off Kilkenny in an All-Ireland final and the Offaly loss was a huge disappointment, obviously, but the positive memories stick.

That Munster final in 2000 wasn't my best-ever game for Cork – it was a decent performance and to contribute was great but it was just about the whole occasion.

It wasn't the best Munster final ever but I'd like to think that it went down as a good game with some special moments.

RONAN CURRAN
(& WAYNE SHERLOCK)

CORK 1-18 CLARE 0-10
Munster SHC Semi-Final
Semple Stadium
JUNE 8, 2003

Defeating Clare so brilliantly in 2003 drove Ronan Curran and Cork to Munster success – here he celebrates with Diarmuid O'Sullivan after defeating Waterford at Semple Stadium.

★ **CORK:** D Óg Cusack; **W Sherlock**, P Mulcahy, D O'Sullivan (0-1); T Kenny, **R Curran**, S Óg Ó hAilpín; M O'Connell (0-1), J Gardiner (0-1); T McCarthy (0-1), N McCarthy (0-2), B O'Connor (0-1); S Ó hAilpín (0-3), J Deane (1-8), A Browne.

★ **CLARE:** D Fitzgerald; B Quinn, B Lohan, F Lohan; C Plunkett (0-1), D McMahon, G Quinn; C Lynch, O Baker; A Markham (0-1), T Griffin, T Carmody (0-3); N Gilligan (0-4), A Quinn, J O'Connor. Subs: B Murphy (0-1) for A Quinn, D O'Connell for Baker, G Considine for Markham, J Reffan for Carmody.

THE ACTION

THE HEADLINE ON the front page of the following day's *Evening Echo* summed it up – *Resurrection Day*.

A disappointing 2002 had culminated with a players' strike that winter, with manager Bertie Óg Murphy an unfortunate casualty. Into the role came Dónal O'Grady, an All-Ireland winner as a player and a selector – and the team for his first championship match saw debuts for Tom Kenny, Ronan Curran and Setanta Ó hAilpín.

Clare had reached the All-Ireland final the previous year and came into the game on the back of a victory over Tipperary, so this was a major test for Cork, but the game was never really a contest.

The Banner were without defensive talisman Seánie McMahon, but it's unlikely that he would have stemmed the rising Cork tide.

Cork didn't concede until the 21st minute, by which time they had put 1-5 on the board – Joe Deane with an exquisite goal in the 13th minute, doubling home after a driving run from Ben O'Connor. By half-time, it was 1-6 to 0-2 but early in the second-half, Clare gave themselves some hope as three quick-fire Niall Gilligan points brought them to within three, 1-7 to 0-7.

It was only a mirage, though, as Cork stepped on the accelerator again.

Mickey O'Connell was outstanding at midfield for the Rebels, and Deane and the younger Ó hAilpín were constant threats in attack.

Cork's performance was so complete that O'Grady didn't feel the need to introduce any substitute and with impeccable full-back Pat Mulcahy leading a defensive performance that never looked like allowing Clare the sniff of a goal, an 11-point winning margin did not flatter the victors in the slightest.

★★★★★

66

MY CORK CHAMPIONSHIP debut was a while arriving, but the wait was ultimately worth it.

I was a dual minor – I had two years in the hurling and one year in the football, 1999. We beat Kerry in the Munster final but I was shocking the same day. I was marking Tadhg Kennelly and I couldn't keep up with him at all! He was a serious underage player.

I enjoyed football and I enjoyed the competitive side of it, but I loved hurling and I was always more drawn to it.

At home, I'd go out the back and be pucking around for hours but I'd never pick up a football and go kicking it! I wouldn't say I was a hurler playing football, either, because I did put a good bit into it and I felt I had the skill level, but just maybe not what was needed physically, or the speed.

I played three years at under-21 in the hurling, but I never actually played under-21 football – I was on the panel for two years, but I think I was injured both times.

I was brought on to the senior hurling panel the year after minor. Jimmy Barry-Murphy brought me in – it was kind of an extended panel more than anything. There were three other young fellas brought into training with me... Pat Sexton, John Anderson and Eoin Fitzgerald.

We were training but we understood that it was training for the future rather than the present. It was unreal to go in and play alongside fellas that had just won an All-Ireland.

I spent my childhood idolising Brian Corcoran and I was there training with him, it was a dream to me. I obviously knew I wasn't ready – I think now, when you come out of minor you have a bit of a chance but, back then, it normally took a few years to get into it. It was great for me, going down to train with the lads and seeing the extra effort levels needed for inter-county.

I was on the panel in 2000, '01 and '02, and I only played one league game in that time; I think it was against Derry at home. I'll be honest, I was getting fairly fed up by the second or third year in there, not getting games.

I walked away at one stage.

I think it was during Tom Cashman's reign, but I came back – I got a couple of phone calls saying I was still very young.

It was still very hard, down there year after year as a young fella and not getting a chance. The most annoying thing for me back then was that Brian was injured, along with a few others, and it ended up with John Browne playing at centre-back.

I'm good friends with John but he used to mock me, saying he was Blackrock's fifth-choice centre-back – he was more of a full-back line player – but he was still getting on ahead of me! Looking back at it, it probably couldn't have worked out better because I came in at a time when things were on the up rather than when they hadn't been so great a few years beforehand.

I was peripheral to the first strike in 2002.

I was still very young and I wouldn't have seen most of the things that had been going on. I didn't know what way that strike was going to go or whatever but, afterwards, it probably benefited me in that Dónal O'Grady came in as a new manager and freshened things up.

Tom Kenny, Setanta Ó hAilpín and I started that year, and John Gardiner and Niall McCarthy had been there the year before. We were going with a younger team and it was the start of a few good years, so it worked out well for us.

Dónal said to me, 'You've always been centre-back, there's a No 6 position there to be won. It's up to you... so off you go'.

I played a few challenge games and did okay. Then it came to the league and I was very lucky to get off to a good start. In my first game against Limerick, I remember playing really well and that gave me the confidence that I was able for that level.

That could very easily go the other way, where a few things go wrong for you and you end up questioning yourself. You can be lucky or unlucky with these things... you don't get too many chances in the backline.

I was fortunate the way things panned out.

I loved centre-back, but it's funny, I played a bit at wing-back in challenge games prior to that and, I'll be honest, I found the wing a lot easier than centre-back!

I preferred the centre – I was obsessed with centre-back and looking at Seánie McMahon and Brian Corcoran and players like that. I used to go to games and zone in on those guys, and nearly forget the rest of it because I just loved everything about the centre-back position.

There was so much to it – it wasn't just beating your man, it was covering the centre, getting in behind your wing-backs, covering midfield. I used to mock John and Seán Óg and have a laugh with them, saying that anyone could play wing-back!

Later on, I did play a few games wing-back in 2006. Obviously, I had a few bad games in 2005 and they decided to switch myself and John for the league and, I'll be honest, I loved it. I thought there was a fierce freedom there and a lot more space to do your hurling, whereas in the centre people are coming from all angles and it's that bit tougher.

When it's going well, it's the best position to play in but when things are tough, it's probably the hardest. I wouldn't say that I couldn't play wing-back – I would have liked it – but centre-back was always my spot and it was where I wanted to be.

I always felt, playing at centre-back, you just had to take care of your man at the start, stick tight to him or whatever, and then play yourself into the game a bit more as it opens up for you… read the game a small bit more.

It's important that the centre-forward doesn't get a good start – I always felt it was like a chess game in that, if you began well and got your hands on the ball, he'd have to start following you a bit more.

Obviously, Brian had been outstanding at centre-back, but I wouldn't say I picked his brains when we were on the panel together because everyone is different and he was the kind of fella who led by performance out on the pitch more than anything. I watched him so closely for years that I knew everything about what he did and, so, I used to model what I did on that and try to get some way near what that man did but, in my opinion, he's the best player to have ever played with Cork… he nearly beat teams on his own.

It was great to be in a dressing-room with him for a few years and see what he did and stuff like that. Then, obviously, to get him back in later years, when he played full-forward, was unbelievable as well.

I think one of the reasons that the Munster Championship game against Clare in 2003 ended up working out so well was that people were unsure beforehand.

We didn't know how good or bad we were; the supporters didn't know how good or bad we were, the other teams didn't know how good or bad we were. Clare had been in the All-Ireland final the year before so they were one of the stronger teams – even though they had a few older lads, they were still serious names.

We were obviously a young team coming in then so maybe there was... I wouldn't say fear on the part of the players, but you're wondering if you're up to the level. It was going to be a test physically... *Would we be up to that?*

There was just that uncertainty between players and supporters, an eerie feeling that it could go either way. Would it be something new or great, or would we be a group of young lads who were told... 'This is senior county hurling, back in your box now!'

You never know with lads making their senior championship debuts – league is grand but championship, there's a shock to it at the start, to get up to the pace of the game.

We all have small pre-game rituals, where we sit and what we do and all that kind of stuff. Going into that game, I had another little thing as I was marking Tony Griffin.

I actually marked him in the Munster minor final in 1998... I was corner-back in that game and he was corner-forward, though I was no more a corner-back than Ben O'Connor! I just hated the spot and, to be fair, on the day he took me to the cleaners.

He had a lot of pace, so that was one thing for me.

I was thinking about him and how I was going to deal with him, because he was a very good player, as he showed in later years. You're always a bit nervous before a big game, but I was more thinking of my man and what I was going to do and that probably helped me to focus my mind... trying to get the better of him, especially in the first 10 minutes.

I always tried to do a lot of research on the fellas I was playing against.

Where they liked to turn.

If they took the man on.

Whether or not they went far out the pitch.

You have to do a bit of that, though these days it might be a bit different in that you could end up marking someone different every 10 minutes. Back then, you had a man to mark and you were fairly sure who it would be, most of the time.

Dónal brought a level of detail that I hadn't seen before. He's very much about the basics and defending... defending from the full-forward line back.

Hooking, blocking, flicking... use of possession was very big with him. I look back on videos now and it's hard to see it because the game has evolved so much in terms of ball-retention over the last few years.

Back then, it was totally new.

Before Dónal came in, it was a case of turn and get rid of the ball as fast as you can... up to the forwards. He was always of the opinion to give it to the right player – give the easy ball, find a man.

We had players like that as well. Jerry O'Connor, Tom Kenny, Ben... players who liked to run with the ball or support the man who had it.

Things fell into place in a way with his style and he probably brought his style on to these players, as well. It suited them and it suited Dónal.

I would have never run with the ball but I was quite happy to lay it off to the likes of Ben or Jerry, for them to run with it. He brought all of that stuff, the art of defending and playing as a team, and he was just very detailed in his analysis. I don't think I ever did video analysis before Dónal.

He'd always have three or four clips before training... 'Look, did you see that? That's what you did there and it didn't work; here, you did it the right way'.

Those things stick in your mind.

He brought a whole new package to it.

I loved playing in Thurles from the start.

I had never experienced anything like the noise, and you could feel the Cork crowd, the wave of excitement when things were going well.

We had a good start and Joe got a goal.

We played well and there are some games where you know you're over the opposition. We felt it that way and we just played good hurling. Tom Kenny had a stormer at wing-back and Wayne was very good in the corner.

We played well all day and ran away with it in the end against a Clare team that had some great players.

We won the game well, so we could enjoy the last 10 minutes of it. Hearing *The Banks* trying to be sung – brutally! – by everyone up on the terrace, there was a feeling of 'newness' to it and you could enjoy it.

We played with an energy that Cork hadn't played with in a few years.

For all those reasons, it was a great game and just a great feeling. There aren't many of those games where you can actually enjoy the last few minutes. We were lucky enough that we could that day, and look forward to what would be coming next.

We went on to win Munster with a great win over that Waterford team. It's funny, the 2004 final is always spoken of as a great game but the 2003 final was too – I don't know if it's because Waterford won 2004 that it gets mentioned more!

We made it to the All-Ireland final against Kilkenny, but we had an awful start to the game. We came back in the second-half and probably could have won it but, maybe, just lacked that bit of experience.

Kilkenny knew how to win, but we weren't there yet.

In saying that, you don't know what might have happened after if we had won in 2003. Now, we lost Setanta, who was one of the biggest-ever losses to Cork hurling, the way he was playing.

That was a loss but obviously we got Brian back, so it's swings and roundabouts.

Those things turn out their own way and it definitely drove us on, and we were a better team in 2004 and '05 because of it.

WAYNE SHERLOCK

Wayne Sherlock races away from Adrian Fenlon and Rory Jacob of Wexford in the 2003 All-Ireland semi-final, but that amazing season got off to the perfect start with a thundering win over Clare.

"

OBVIOUSLY, WE WON the All-Ireland in 1999, which was my first year.

When you're young, you're trying not to get carried away with things so you're just taking it game by game.

After that, in 2000 we under-achieved; we fell flat on our faces against Offaly, and then we had a couple of barren years.

I was captain in 2002 and we all know what happened that year, with the strike and all of that hassle. Then, into 2003, it wasn't that we were trying to prove anything, because we knew we were good enough, but that doesn't mean that you're going to perform.

The Clare game stands out for me because it was like a release... *We have to perform and we have to show people that all we care about is hurling; nothing else.*

If we didn't perform in that game, we'd probably have been slated and I think everything clicked that day. Coming off the field, the feeling was relief… that we could still do it.

We knew that it was the start of something.

I don't speak much after games, but in April, after we beat Clare in the league in Ennis, I said to the lads that I had a good feeling – if we believed in ourselves and kept doing the hard work, that something special would happen.

We knew that if we got off to a good start, we'd build and build… and BUILD.

I started playing for Blackrock at under-6 level – we used to walk from Mahon up to Blackrock and it felt like a long walk! One of the parents, Michael Lucey, used to bring a good eight or nine of us up on a Saturday morning, taking a shortcut through the convent to get to Church Road.

It was like a massive pilgrimage!

They were great days. Blackrock had huge tradition and history, obviously, but I actually didn't know many of these big names because my parents didn't come from a GAA background and they didn't go to games when I was growing up.

I wouldn't say I went in blind – I would have heard names and things like that, and Pat Moylan coached me from under-12 to minor – but I didn't really get to know them until I got older. I went to Blackrock because all of my friends were going there.

Adrian Coughlan and Barry Henneberry were the players that I looked up to. They were on Cork under-14 and Cork under-16 teams and then, when I got up to senior, it was Fergal Ryan and John Browne.

Did I realise I could go to a high level?

I just kept playing – I suppose, I always felt that I was trying to prove myself. I never relaxed and thought… *I'm after making it here.*

It was about going out again to perform and perform… and PERFORM.

I was lucky in that I was on a Seandún (city division) under-16 team that won the Munster regional tournament. There were great players on that team like Mark Prendergast and Stephen O'Connell, but I never felt that I was in the same bracket as them.

Then I was a Cork minor after Blackrock won the county, so I was getting a taste of winning every year and they were all stepping stones. I didn't even have time to think about it, I was just trying to make the team that I was on.

When you win something, it gives you confidence and you enjoy the feeling that comes with it.

Cork won the All-Ireland under-21 in 1997.

I was on that team and there were a good few of us under-age again in 1998. There were a few senior trial games after 1997 but I came back at the start of '98 and I had taken my eye off the ball and I wasn't a bit fit.

Bertie Óg Murphy was the under-21 manager and he pulled me aside in around March after we played the Cork seniors in a challenge match.

'Wayne!' he said, 'You need to lose a stone. You're absolutely way out of shape.' From that moment, I got unbelievably fit.

I trained with the club and trained on my own twice a day.

We won the under-21 again that year, and Blackrock made it to the county final in November, so my fitness stayed up until late into the year. Then Jimmy Barry-Murphy brought me into the Cork set-up for 1999 and having that base of fitness really helped me. If Bertie Óg hadn't had those words, maybe I'd have stayed unfit for a bit longer and then struggled, so it was definitely the kick in the ass that I needed at the time.

It was an important learning curve for me.

The pace was a noticeable step up at senior, but at the same time, you're used to marking good players from under-21 and winning an All-Ireland helps too in terms of giving you confidence. Before the start of the Munster Senior Championship in 1999, Brian Corcoran said to us, 'Ye've no baggage... Limerick or Clare or Waterford have never beaten ye'.

So, while Clare had beaten Cork at senior in 1993, '95, '97 and '98, those of us from the under-21s didn't fear them before the Munster final, even though they were going for three in-a-row.

After winning the under-21 All-Ireland in 1997, Bertie Óg said to us in the dressing-room after, 'The last time Cork won the under-21 (1988), they won the senior two years later!' Even somebody just saying that, something clicked for fellas.

It was something he didn't have to say but, all of a sudden, we're thinking... *You never know.*

When we won the All-Ireland in 1999, I was No 5, as I had been throughout the championship. In league games that year, I was playing corner-back, so to be named right half-back for the championship match against Waterford was a bit of a shock to me, to be honest – even though I played left half-back for Blackrock in my first senior year and I loved it.

I injured my hamstring a month before the Waterford game and I struggled to get back, but I did well then in a challenge match against Tipperary at the opening of a pitch. I think Derek Barrett had been meant to play right half-back that day but he got injured, and I came in.

It was between me, Barrett and Johnny Sheehan, and I was lucky enough to get the chance and I grabbed it with both hands.

It was a bit of a shock, but I had Brian Corcoran beside me, and Fergal Ryan beside me, so I was in good company.

We only conceded one goal in the four matches we played to win the 1999 All-Ireland. We all loved defending, which is something that we tried to instil in the Cork under-20s when I was involved with them… you have to love it.

We were going to do anything to stop whoever we were playing against.

Myself, Sully, Seán Óg, Dónal Óg and John Browne had under-21 medals, and then you had Brian Corcoran and Fergal… we were really close as a bunch.

In 2002, I was captain.

While there was a messy end, that didn't really put extra pressure on me more than anything else. I loved every bit about being captain – I actually thrived on it and really enjoyed being in that position.

I was captain of Blackrock for three or four years and I really loved it. I'm not one for big speeches, it's more about trying to be as consistent as you can. You've a sense of trying to lead by example on the pitch.

You're trying to show that attitude in matches and training, and it really appealed to me.

Bertie Óg was the senior manager that year.

He gave me and so many other guys a chance and his whole thing was, 'We've got to win a senior'. He wasn't there to be selfish and just focus on winning the under-21; from the start, it was about developing players for senior.

Players would have done anything for Bertie Óg and he just got stuck in the middle of that situation. It was a shame, it had nothing to do with him.

If I was to change one thing, I'd liked to have won a senior All-Ireland with him because I think he deserved it. It was definitely one of the things I feel bad about. We lost to Kilkenny by a point in the league final in 2002; if we had won that, then things might have been different.

Dónal O'Grady came in for 2003 and he brought brilliant discipline to it.

He saw that we had under-achieved for a few years, even allowing for us winning Munster in 2000. He knew that he had fellas there to do it and he wasn't going to leave until he got the job done.

He brought back the basics.

Maybe, at that time, senior county teams assumed that all players could do the basics and do them well, but you'd be very surprised.

Dónal made fellas do the basics well and he was there to witness it – he didn't just tell us to go away and do it ourselves. The way he saw it was, that if you did the simple things right, the rest would look after itself.

In terms of a routine leading up to a game, I always loved pucking a ball against the wall and would do that as I much as I could in the week before.

I might try to have the same food if I'd played well after eating a particular dinner, wear the same shorts and socks maybe, but at the same time you're trying not to get too caught up in that. These things are just mind games that you're playing with yourself – anything that you can think of that might have made you play well the last time, you're trying to do it again! That's why journals are all the go these days, so players don't forget anything.

I used to generally try to sit in the same seat on the bus or in the dressing-room and so did most fellas, so when we're all doing it, it just fits together like a jigsaw! It made everyone feel normal and relaxed.

I was marking Barry Murphy that day in 2003.

As the years went on, we were given videos and DVDs of players; but, to be honest, I never, ever looked at one of them. In my head, I felt that if I focused on it too much – whether a guy pucked off his left or right or whatever – you're nearly over-thinking it and second-guessing yourself.

I just wanted to play off the cuff.

I know some fellas loved it and felt they got a lot of help from it. There are pluses and minuses to these things but I didn't feel comfortable doing it, to be honest. I actually like the video analysis of teams and what they'd do, but I never looked at any of the individual players I'd be marking.

I just wanted to go out fresh and say… *Let's see who can get to the ball first.*

I presume the public were divided after the strike; no matter what the circumstances are, you're never going to get one hundred percent of people supporting you.

But we knew that we just wanted to play hurling and I think we proved that by going on to reach four All-Ireland finals in-a-row.

We had to show that we weren't side-tracked by what had gone on.

Cork people are very good at letting you know how they feel. That's what I've found with Cork teams – if you get beaten by 10 points but give it your all and make an unbelievable effort, the Cork public will absolutely clap you on the back and say, 'Well done, you tried, you tried, you tried.'

But if you go out and there are fellas not making an effort, that's not accepted. Cork people expect big performances, whether you win or lose – just keep going, whatever the score is.

I was a selector with the under-20s the last two years and that's what we said to them… if you keep trying and putting the effort in whether you're winning or losing, you'll earn respect and the public will come and follow you. It was something that was bred into us, really.

We won by 1-18 to 0-10 and the Cork fans singing *The Banks*… that stood out a mile. When you're in Croke Park, people ask if you can hear 82,000 people… and you can, but you can't! You're in the zone, though that's probably a cliché.

That day, we were a good bit ahead and, for whatever reason, we could hear that singing. Even thinking back, the hairs still stand on the back of the neck.

When we won a game in Thurles, walking through town to go back to the hotel was brilliant. Back in 1999 and 2000, no matter how good the players were – Brian Corcoran, Joe Deane and all these fellas – when you're walking through Thurles the crowd are shouting for Jimmy.

It would make you feel so proud that he was your manager.

We didn't have that walk for a few years and, so, to have it again in 2003 was brilliant.

99

KIERAN MURPHY

CORK 2-19 TIPPERARY 1-16
All-Ireland SHC Qualifier Round 2
Fitzgerald Stadium
JULY 10, 2004

Cork got back on track in 2004 by defeating Tipperary in Killarney, and the game of Kieran Murphy's life set them up for All-Ireland success – here he chases away from Kilkenny's Derek Lyng and Ken Coogan in the final.

★ **CORK:** D Óg Cusack; W Sherlock, D O'Sullivan, B Murphy; J Gardiner (0-1), R Curran, S Óg Ó hAilpín; T Kenny, J O'Connor (0-1); B O'Connor (0-4), N McCarthy (1-2), G McCarthy; **K Murphy (0-2)**, B Corcoran, J Deane (0-7). Subs: T McCarthy (1-1) for G McCarthy, M O'Connell (0-1) for Kenny.

★ **TIPPERARY:** B Cummins; M Maher, P Maher, P Curran; E Corcoran, D Fanning, D Fitzgerald; C Morrissey (0-1), T Dunne; P Kelly (1-0), C Gleeson (0-1), B Dunne (0-3); E Kelly (0-9), J Carroll (0-1), S Butler. Subs: L Corbett for Butler, M O'Leary (0-1) for P Kelly, N Morris for Carroll.

THE ACTION

EVER SINCE 1987 and the Munster final replay, 'Killarney' was a shorthand for Tipperary's re-emergence as big players on the national scene and, so, when Fitzgerald Stadium was chosen for this qualifier tie, there was a sense that it benefited the Premier County.

Both sides had lost to Waterford – Tipp in the Munster semi-final, and Cork in the epic provincial decider – leading to them being drawn together in the All-Ireland series for the first time.

While it was Cork's turn to host based on the counties' home-and-away arrangement, Tipp argued that that only applied for Munster Championship games and, so, the Cork hurling faithful had the novelty of the trip west that was usually only made for football games against Kerry.

Such was the traffic congestion in trying to reach the tourist destination on a mid-July Saturday, that throw-in was delayed for a quarter of an hour.

When the match did finally get going, it was Tipp who settled better as they moved into a 0-7 to 0-2 lead inside the opening 14 minutes. And, while Cork were back within a point as half-time approached, Paul Kelly's goal – a rebound after his brother Eoin's penalty was saved by Dónal Óg Cusack – ensured that it was 1-8 to 0-7 for Ken Hogan's side.

A skirmish before the break had served to jolt Cork and, on the resumption, they turned the game. Timmy McCarthy, on as a first-half sub, scored a goal that was the centrepiece of an unanswered 1-3. Though Tipp didn't lead again, they were back to within a point with seven minutes left as Eoin Kelly led their charge.

However, Cork's second goal, scored by Niall McCarthy, put the issue beyond doubt and they had four of the last five points.

Antrim fell to the Rebels in the All-Ireland quarter-finals, while Dónal O'Grady's side overcame Leinster champions Wexford in the semis. The final would be a repeat of 2003, Cork up against a Kilkenny side that had also come through the back door, but the outcome was different as a 0-17 to 0-9 victory saw Cork claim the Liam MacCarthy Cup for the 29th time.

★★★★★

66

AT THE START of 2004, I remember Dónal O'Grady calling me aside and telling me that I was going to get a lot of runs in the league. 'You'll be given the opportunity, so make sure you work hard and do you your best'.

It was a simple message like that.

After we had won the minor All-Ireland in 2001, myself, John Gardiner and Setanta Ó hAilpín were brought on to the extended training panel with the seniors to give us a bit of experience. Gardiner managed to make the team, though!

I had been a three-year minor. It gave you that exposure at national level and it was definitely a help for the three of us that we won the minor, but it was still a big step up.

I had turned 19 that February and we played a few in-house games that summer. A lot of the 1999 team were still there and you were going in pucking around before training with the likes of Joe Deane, Seánie McGrath... all of these guys who you would have looked up to.

I remember in one of those games I was marked by Wayne Sherlock and he gave me a bit of a lesson. When I was coming off, I was talking to Seánie and he said, 'Don't worry about it, Sherlock destroys us all!'

That was a good learning experience and it got me used to the senior county environment, what training was like and what was expected.

It was an eye-opener as to how top players operated.

Normally, when you were a young fella, you were going down and just pucking around before training, whereas now, I was going down and I was watching fellas do gym sessions beforehand. Pat Ryan, who's from Sars too, was still there and I used to pal around with him; he'd be practising his frees beforehand.

There was always a purpose to what people were doing.

Dónal came in at the start of 2003, and Seánie O'Leary was there, too – he obviously would have known me well, as Tomás is the same age and captained the 2001 minor team. It was Seánie who gave me the call to say that I was part of the official panel.

We used to train down in Ballygarvan a lot. At minor level, we would have done a bit of physical training with Denis Ring, but the stuff with Seánie McGrath was the first proper pre-season training that I would have done. It was a massive adjustment and even the way Seánie was doing the training was different to what a lot of the guys were used to, anyway.

There was a change for everyone but it was fairly brutal.

You'd be going from Seánie over to Dónal, who was doing a lot of work on tackling and hooking and blocking. There was a big emphasis on the basics, but I just remember it being so tough.

I played a few of the league games and would have come on a good bit. Then, in the championship, I came on in the All-Ireland semi-final replay against Wexford. One of the things at which Dónal was excellent was that, when you were on the bench, he always made you feel like you had a role to play.

In hindsight, I mightn't have had much real chance of making an impact that year but you'd always feel you could. It was great when they gave me the opportunity to come on against Wexford.

I can remember one high ball coming in and I went to grab it, but a defender, I think it was Declan Ruth, cleaned me. It was a real eye-opener because you had a six-foot-four man coming across you and it gave me a real insight into the physicality and speed of senior hurling at that level.

It was a great experience, especially when we were winning and going into an All-Ireland final. It was a real high to be coming on, even if it was just for five minutes.

The final defeat in 2003 was tough and, after coming on in the semi-final replay, you were disappointed not to get a run in the final. Realistically, it might have been too early. Being part of the final was a great experience and all that, but it's a massive blow when you lose.

I played a good few games in the league in 2004.

I remember we played Clare down in Páirc Uí Rinn and I was marking Gerry O'Grady, who was one of their main defenders at the time. I played well that day and Dónal came up to me after and said, 'That's what we want, you're in pole position now!'

The management were always good to give positive feedback, which is great.

In the championship, we played Kerry first and then Limerick in the semi-final, but before that, I got injured playing an Intermediate Football Championship game for Glanmire. I broke a finger on my right hand, so that put me out for four or five weeks.

That obviously was a tough blow for me as I had been going well and, now, I was going to have a spell off the field, only able to do physical training and not being able to play.

Throughout my career, I missed very few championship games with injury and it was frustrating that that one came at the start.

I travelled up to Limerick with the team but I wasn't togged or anything, and I remember sitting in the stand, feeling disappointed. I was pleased the lads were going well, obviously, but I'd have loved to have been out there myself.

We had lost Setanta after 2003 – he went to Australia – but Brian Corcoran came back for 2004 and it gave us a huge boost. Even though Brian's a very quiet fella, when he walked back in for his first training session, it was one of those things that takes everybody's attention. He just has that aura about him.

He had played a couple of league games with Erin's Own and it was rumoured that he was thinking of coming back with Cork, so when he did it was great. With Brian, there was no big drama or anything like that – he came in, togged off, chatted to a few of the lads and then went out training and headed home.

That's just the type of guy he is, it's why he's a great leader.

Waterford beat us in a Munster final that's still talked about but there's no real consolation in losing a classic. We started off well, but Paul Flynn's famous goal from a free was a bit of a turning point as it gave them a real lift. It was very disappointing.

I had only been back training about two weeks before that so I didn't start, which was a small bit disappointing, but I came on with a few minutes to go. I remember a high ball coming in and I broke it down, and I picked it.

I just recall Jerry O'Connor steaming through, off my shoulder.

I didn't see him, I only heard him shouting, so I went to pop it to him. He put out his hand to grab it but, just at the last second, Declan Prendergast threw a hurley at it and flicked it away. It was just one of those things – if the ball went to hand, it was a certain goal but they went up the field and got a point.

The fact that we got Tipp in the qualifier draw focused minds fairly quickly, definitely. I remember after that Munster final, we had a chat. The feeling was that, while we wanted to win Munster, what we were really going for that year was the All-Ireland.

We were in that system now.

It was felt at the time that, because of the home-and-away arrangement, it was our turn to play Tipp down the Páirc but they were objecting to it, saying that the arrangement was only for Munster Championship games. They insisted on it going to Fitzgerald Stadium. I don't know how true it was or if Dónal was using it for motivation, but the message was that Tipp saw a weakness in us if they got us out of the Páirc.

We weren't pinning it up on the wall, but it was something that would have been spoken about.

We went down to Killarney the week before the game and we trained, because it was a bit of a concern that so many of us would have been unfamiliar with it, and the playing surface wasn't great at that particular time. Dónal brought the team down doing scenario work on one side of the field and I went down to get involved in that, but he called me aside and said, 'Here's 10 sliothars. Go up into the right corner and start shooting points'.

Going up the field, I felt disappointed because I thought I wasn't going to be part of the plans for the following weekend but little did I know that he wanted to see how I did with the under-21s during the week.

It was a challenge game and I was the only senior playing as he wanted me to get match-fitness. He didn't say that to me at the time, but he was at the game and I remember thinking that it was strange. He came up to me afterwards and said that he wanted to see me in a match. The team for the Tipp game was named on the Thursday and I got a call beforehand to say that I'd be starting.

The pre-match routine was something that I'd have been used to for a few years at that stage but obviously it was totally different for that game.

It was mid-summer, so peak tourism time in Killarney, and a lot of people were giving out about the throw-in time of 4.15pm. We travelled down on the bus and we didn't have an escort at the time – we just came around a corner and the traffic was literally bumper to bumper... like a car park.

The bus turned around and we were going down boreens to get there, but we arrived at the stadium a lot later than we normally would.

There was a bit of a rush and then the announcement came that the game was going to be delayed because so many supporters were late. It was a bit chaotic, but Brian Corcoran called everyone into the dressing-room and said, 'Look lads, we're here to do a job – whatever time they want us to play, we'll play. Let's just keep the focus'.

In other venues, you'd always have your spot in the dressing-room but, obviously, not having played in Fitzgerald Stadium, you wouldn't. The only real ritual I had was that I liked to have a ball in my hand coming out on to the pitch, just for that first strike. At places where you'd play a lot, you might have a few other routines.

I was marking Paul Curran, someone I had marked in the Fitzgibbon Cup. I think it was his second year with Tipp as well but he had played a few games in 2003. He was a very good defender and I got to know him after, when we played together with Munster in the Railway Cup. He's a sound fella, but that day there was a bit of needle because it was such a high-stakes game for both counties.

Previously, when I was going to Cork games with my buddy Johnny Crowley, we used to always have a bit of a bet between ourselves as to who'd get the first score. After about 10 seconds, the ball was in our right half-back position and John Gardiner got it and he broke out from defence.

From years of playing with John, I knew his habits and his style, and I saw him cut into the centre on his left-hand side. Whenever John did that, he always played the ball into the right-hand corner – it was his natural strike.

I knew it was coming as soon as he turned to his left, so I just went.

It was a great ball in, one bounce and into the hand. I turned then and faced up to Paul Curran and I kind of jinked off my right leg and on to the left one, into the centre. I hit off my left and it looked like it was going to go wide for a while, but it just kind of tailed in at the last second.

It was a dream start, to get your first championship point like that in the first minute. I remember saying to Crowley afterwards that I hoped he had a bet with someone on me to get the first score! It was at the same end that Dónal O'Grady had sent me to, and he came up to me after the game and said, 'You were kind of half-sulking last week because you thought I was just sending you away!'

We had a good laugh about it.

Scoring early like that just gives you that bit of confidence, the affirmation that you're here and you can deliver. As well, it just confirmed that I was back up to the pace of things.

In the first-half, we went 0-7 to 0-2 down and I remember Ben O'Connor roaring in to keep taking our points. We came back, but Tipp got a penalty and we actually saved it only for them to get a goal from the rebound.

After that, under the covered stand, Benny Dunne had a wild swing on Jerry; you'd probably get sent off for it these days but Barry Kelly only gave a yellow for it.

What it did was, it led to even more tension and aggression.

Straight after that, Jerry O'Connor made a great run through the centre and put the ball over the bar... so it gave us a big lift, even though we were going in behind. It was a case of... *If ye want to fight, we'll fight... if ye want to play, we'll play.*

Timmy McCarthy had been dropped after the Munster final but he was brought on for the second-half and had an immediate impact. Niall Mac went for a shot that was half-blocked and Timmy picked it up, and buried it. I was inside and had peeled away for the hand-pass, but he was just so fired up that day when he came on that he just saw the goal.

Brendan Cummins didn't even see it.

Then Niall got a goal that was kind of a rehearsed move in one sense.

It was a long puckout that went down on Brian Corcoran, and then it was about the fella coming on to the break. The first one or two didn't work out, but I remember Brian coming over to me and saying to come around in front for the next long one.

When he tells you that, you do it!

The ball came in and Brian went as if he was going to pull on it but, at the last second, he put up his hurley and blocked it in front. I ran around and I picked it, and all I heard was Niall Mac roaring... 'FRAGGIE, FRAGGIE... FRAGGIE!'

I looked up and he was about 30 yards away so I hand-passed it as far as I could, but it was just short of him and was bobbling on. He went to pick it and missed it, but it was just one of those where it was on the half-bounce and he just connected with it... a sweet strike off his left.

That put us four up and gave us daylight. The crowd was just unbelievable down there. It was definitely four-to-one in terms of Cork supporters against Tipp and the roar when Niall got the goal was huge.

He threw his hurley about 60 yards into the air as well!

We won by six in the end and it felt like the season was back on track. I got a second point too, so it was great for me in that it started well and finished well.

When we came back into the dressing-room, it was just unbelievable. You were just fighting past fellas to get in. It was such a tense game... the delayed start, the big fight... having to go down to Killarney.

There was huge pressure on both teams and, I suppose, we felt that we had more to offer in the championship. It was just about winning more than anything and relief afterwards. It being a Saturday evening down in Killarney, I remember walking around afterwards and there was a great atmosphere.

We were disappointed after losing the 2003 All-Ireland final and then the 2004 Munster final, but that game really gave us our confidence and our mojo back, and set us on the way to win the All-Ireland.

TOM KENNY

CORK 1-21   GALWAY 1-16
All-Ireland SHC Final
Croke Park
SEPTEMBER 11, 2005

Tom Kenny beats Fergal Healy of Galway in the 2005 All-Ireland final.

★ **CORK:** D Óg Cusack; P Mulcahy, D O'Sullivan, B Murphy; J Gardiner (0-1), R Curran, S Óg Ó hAilpín; J O'Connor (0-2), **T Kenny (0-3)**; T McCarthy (0-2), N McCarthy (0-1), Kieran 'Fraggie' Murphy; B O'Connor (1-7), B Corcoran (0-2), J Deane (0-3). Subs: N Ronan for K Murphy, Kieran 'Hero' Murphy for N McCarthy.

★ **GALWAY:** L Donoghue; D Joyce, T Óg Regan, O Canning; D Hardiman (0-1), S Kavanagh, D Collins; D Tierney (0-1), F Healy (0-2); R Murphy, D Forde, A Kerins (0-3); G Farragher (0-8), N Healy (0-1), D Hayes (1-0). Subs: K Broderick for N Healy, K Hayes for Forde.

THE ACTION

WHILE DÓNAL O'GRADY had stepped down after the All-Ireland win of 2004, John Allen's accession to the role from selector had been seamless, and Cork had impressed in winning Munster before having to show all of their character in coming from behind to beat Clare in the All-Ireland semi-final.

Brian Corcoran and Ronan Curran had been substituted in that triumph over the Banner but both showed in the final that such displays were only blips. Corcoran excelled as Cork moved ahead, 0-4 to 0-1 after 10 minutes, while Curran and captain Seán Óg Ó hAilpín dictated matters in the half-back line. Ben O'Connor's goal in the 16th minute, made possible by a long Diarmuid O'Sullivan clearance, opened up a six-point lead and there appeared to be little possibility of Galway reproducing the form that had seen them down Kilkenny in a titanic semi-final.

The Tribesmen began to come into the game more as half-time neared, however, driven on by Ollie Canning and Tony Óg Regan in defence, while David Tierney tried to break up the supremacy enjoyed by Tom Kenny and Jerry O'Connor in midfield for Cork. Tierney and partner Fergal Healy each had a point while Ger Farragher punished Cork indiscretion with converted frees – and the deficit was down to just two, 1-9 to 0-10, by the interval.

But Cork's belief was never shaken and they pushed ahead again early in the second-half, with Timmy McCarthy's superb point personifying their confidence and composure. They led by 1-14 to 0-13 in the 49th minute, when Galway struck for a goal, Damien Hayes reacting quickest after a good Dónal Óg Cusack save to deny Richie Murray.

It was the pivotal period of the whole game, but Galway were never able to achieve parity and Cork ensured that they would not be caught. Kenny and Jerry O'Connor both had points as the Rebels regained a midfield foothold while Ben O'Connor added to a personal tally that would see him finish with 1-8.

A memorable occasion was capped as Ó hAilpín, born in Fiji and who first picked up a hurley at the age of 11, delivered his acceptance speech entirely in Irish.

★★★★★

"

I WAS TURNING 22 when I played my first game for Cork, which was probably old to be making your debut!

I came on to the panel under Dónal O'Grady when he was appointed before the 2003 season. I had been knocking around the place in the year or two before that, but I wasn't anywhere near making the team or panel. I suppose I wasn't developed enough, firstly, and I wouldn't have been able to perform to that level, really.

By 2003, I was on the hurling and football panels, and playing a bit for both. Dónal gave me my first hurling start in a league match against Tipperary up in Thurles around Easter weekend and it took off from there.

I made my championship debut that summer.

At the time, Grenagh were a junior hurling club but I had gone to secondary school in Farranferris and then on to UCC – my decision to go there was largely centred around getting exposure in the Fitzgibbon Cup, with a view to playing for Cork down the road.

I knew that I wouldn't have been able to play senior inter-county at 18, 19 or 20. John Gardiner played at 19 but he was exceptional, whereas I knew that I wasn't nearly ready enough.

I think the three or four years playing Fitzgibbon Cup and coming up against players from outside of Cork gave me a good grounding.

It didn't bother me that I was that bit older before I played – I just saw that as a natural progression for me at that stage.

In fairness to Dónal, too, he took a punt in 2003 – I think a few of us made our debuts together that day. He would have been very much a coach who put a lot of importance on the skills of the game and not just necessarily being able to get the ball and hit it down the field. If he could see that you were able to tackle properly or hook properly or block properly, he could see you bringing something to the game for the team.

My early days were focused on that; I was able to tackle and hook and cover ground, and that gave me the confidence then, as the matches went on and the years went on, to progress my game more.

I started at wing-back and played there all through 2003 and the early part of '04, when we played Limerick in the Gaelic Grounds in the Munster quarter-final. I was doing my final-year college exams at the time and I was training and studying away, and feeling grand, but it's only when you play a championship match that you realise how much sitting down and studying takes out of you!

I played okay in the first-half but I wouldn't say that I was myself.

I remember Dónal asking me at half-time if I was alright, and I said that I was grand and had my second breath and was in the game.

He could have easily taken me off but he gave me that second chance and I was swapped with John Gardiner; he went to wing-back and I went to midfield. John had started there with Mickey O'Connell but in the second-half I was moved in there and so was Jerry O'Connor, who started at wing-forward.

Up to then, Jerry was in and out of the team and it was the first game where we ended up together, and it just took off.

The management saw that we linked well together in terms of helping each other out and getting forward and back when needed, and that obviously helped the team, too. It just snowballed from there and it was the catalyst for the rest of the season.

Equally, John Gardiner really blossomed at wing-back and brought another level to his performances, alongside Ronan Curran and Seán Óg Ó hAilpín.

We won that 2004 All-Ireland through the back door and that obviously gave us huge confidence. Towards the end of that year, I think it was around the middle of December, we trained down in Riverstown.

John Allen had taken over from Dónal and, before we went on the team holiday, he wanted a session or two to lay down the law, as such. John had obviously had his own journey from backroom member to selector up to manager, and he wanted to put his stamp and voice on things.

Seán Óg – who was captain for 2005 as Na Piarsaigh had won the county championship – spoke before that session and said, 'Look, John is the manager now and if he says, "Jump" we ask, "How high?"'

To John's eternal credit as well, he didn't try to change things too much. He saw what was working well and kept those things going but then brought his own voice to the set-up. It's like any Cork team – when you start training at the start of the year, your goal is to win the All-Ireland and you'll forever think you're good enough to do it, whether you've won the previous three or if you haven't won anything for 20 years.

That's probably the way we viewed it.

It was an up-and-down league for us and then we went into the Munster Championship against Waterford at the semi-final stage. We won that by two points and then beat Tipp in the Munster final in Thurles, but it took us a while to properly get going and get into a rhythm.

As the season went on, we got better and performed better.

At the time, there was an expanded quarter-final stage and the provincial champions didn't go straight into an All-Ireland semi-final. We ended up playing Waterford again in the quarter-finals, this time in Croke Park.

They had gone through the back door and played a few games, so they had a bit of an advantage and they played much better for a lot of that game. It took a very good goal from Brian Corcoran to bring us over the line.

Then, in the semi-final against Clare, they had us on the ropes.

We weren't motoring well at all, but John made the decision to bring Ronan Curran and Brian Corcoran off, big calls given the calibre of the players.

We came back to win and it just went to show that John had great faith in the panel and it paid off in those decisions. That was good management and there was speculation that there might be changes for the final but Brian and Ronan had given such great service and performed so brilliantly over the previous couple of years that it was never the case that they weren't going to start. They had built up that credit in terms of performances and ability to win the battles in their positions, and it was good management, too, to stick with them.

It's only now, when I'm finished playing and doing some coaching in my club and with UCC, that I appreciate how you deal with things like that.

We were the first semi-final and Galway played Kilkenny the following weekend. Kilkenny had lost to us in the previous year's final and they were no doubt looking to get back to avenge that, but Galway brought a great level of performance to that game and got some great goals.

I think, in the long run, Kilkenny acknowledged that that game turned their thinking in terms of how they needed to play and how they needed to approach games. On the other hand, it probably opened our eyes a small bit as to what

Galway could bring to the table... *They're after beating Kilkenny in an All-Ireland semi-final by getting so many scores, we need to be really on our game.*

For All-Ireland finals, we used to get the train up from Kent Station in Cork on the Saturday and then get a bus across Dublin from Heuston... meander down the quays and over to The Burlington Hotel. Everyone was relaxed and by the time you got to the hotel it was nearly dinner-time.

Sometimes, people used to go to the cinema but, after the travel, I was just happy going for a walk, down past Herbert Park, Raglan Road, that kind of way. Bishop Buckley would come up and say Mass on the Saturday evening in the hotel. The Premiership would be back up and running after the summer and you'd watch *Match of The Day* before bed.

Sunday morning was always long, though, as you were up early for the breakfast and you had time to kill. It's funny, you'd be sitting in the hotel room watching the minor match and thinking that you'd be out there in a few hours.

But then, once you'd had the pre-match meal at half past 12 or 1 o'clock, you were getting in the zone, getting ready and packing bags. It's funny the things people don't think about – you're coming back to the hotel that night but, whereas on the Saturday night you're rooming with a teammate, you're going to be staying with your partner or wife or whatever on the Sunday... so you're packing up the room you're in and leaving a bag to be put elsewhere for later.

There are a lot of things to be boxed off before you can get tuned into the game.

I could always gauge how I was feeling by the bus trip to the stadium. The streets are busier for the final and you get goosebumps and the hair standing on the back of your neck when you see the people on the way to the match.

If I was getting that, I knew I was in a good place but, very seldom, if I was looking out and taking in everything, I'd know that my head wasn't in the match. That sounds like it's contradicting itself, but it's how it felt to me.

We used to come in at the Cusack Stand side and go around the tunnel to the Hogan Stand side. It was brilliant seeing and hearing the crowd, and it began to tune your mind and focus in on the game.

The fact that we under-performed so much against Clare, I think the management might have recognised that, either (a) we were after getting into a rut and were just going through the motions, or (b) we had become comfortable with our system, to the point that it wasn't challenging us.

John made the decision that we'd play a longer style of game in the final.

We wouldn't run the ball as much and we were told to take scoring chances out the field if we got them – old-school, essentially, though it was 16 years ago so maybe not so old-school back then! It was a case of tweaking our system and it worked out well.

I got a couple of points from out the field, John Gardiner got one and Ben got a lot of scores. Our goal came from a long ball down the field by Diarmuid O'Sullivan.

If you watch the game back, it was very much end-to-end and there wasn't as much running or support play, like we would have done in previous years. I think we might have caught Galway a bit by surprise in doing that – they were expecting a fast game, taking us on one-on-one, whereas we changed it around.

Again, all credit to John for making that decision and seeing the opportunity. Obviously, in hindsight it's a great decision, but when you're making it, you know that it could go either way.

There was some adaptation for me at midfield, but I think I knew how to do that. I always say that you can play midfield and touch the ball four times and score three points, and people will say you had a fantastic game. On another day, you could be on the ball 20 times but be hooked and blocked once or twice and only get on the scoresheet once, and they'll say you had a very quiet game.

It didn't really bother me what people – supporters or reporters or whoever – said outside the camp. Once John, my teammates and my own family and friends knew that I was contributing to the benefit of the team, I was satisfied. Even if that contribution was 'only' making hooks and blocks around the middle of the field and someone else was picking up the ball and getting scores, I was perfectly happy with that.

From that point of view, that game was different in that we were getting the ball around midfield and being told not to run with it, but that wasn't the law, either – you played it as you saw it. I got a few chances to score that day and I took them, but there were other occasions where fellas ran with it and that was fine.

I suppose, it was a bit difficult to get out of the mindset of running up the field and supporting the forwards. You'd still venture back and help out the defence as best you could, but you wouldn't be flat-out going forward. It took a while to get used to, but at that time I was playing the game long enough to understand where I needed to go and what I needed to do.

Our goal came in the first-half, after Diarmuid got the ball and launched it down the field. The Galway centre-back went to play it and missed it, and Ben was running across from the wing or the corner, with Ollie Canning following him, and he got a shot off into the bottom corner.

It was an important score for us at the time and it just edged us three or four points ahead and gave us that space for the rest of the game.

They got a scrappy goal to bring it back to two or three points, but it never felt like we were going to lose. We had their measure and it was just a case of keeping them at arm's length. Even watching the game back during one of the lockdowns, it probably looked scrappy compared to the matches nowadays but we always felt in control.

Maybe that's a bad thing, that we did the work and got the scores when we needed to rather than keeping our foot on the pedal, but I think we were on the road long enough by then to understand how to play the game as a team and to get over the line.

Winning your first All-Ireland is always special, especially after what we had been through. In 2003, we had been riding the crest of a wave and we all expected to go to Dublin and win the All-Ireland, a young team with a huge following.

After losing that and then the Munster final in 2004 against Waterford, to come back and win the All-Ireland, beating Kilkenny, was just brilliant. So the first is probably always better than… I'd love to say 'every other time', but there was only one other time!

What I recall from 2005 is that I was near the referee Séamus Roche when he blew the whistle and I just put my arms in the air… but there was no mad jumping around like in '04.

Brian Carthy from RTÉ interviewed me in the Hogan Stand and that's my main recollection of the period after the whistle.

Seán Óg's speech was go léir trí Gaeilge and that was the other stand-out memory. The dressing-room was a bit of a blur; it's like anything, the time just goes too quickly. Two years previously, when we had been on the losing side, everything seemed to go in slow-motion. Back to the hotel then and the crowd greets you at the banquet – the train journey down on the Monday then is incredible. That is one super highlight.

If you had said to me on that day in September 2005 that Cork wouldn't win another one by 2021, I'd have said you were off your game. The following year, we got to the final but Kilkenny had our measure and it was the beginning of their period of dominance.

I still think that, in the period 2006, '07 and '08, we still probably had a team good enough to win another All-Ireland. There has been a lot of coverage given to what happened then, but I'd like to think that the players who went out, trained and played to their best. There's certainly a tinge of disappointment that we didn't win another All-Ireland after 2005. We got there in 2013 and a last-minute Clare equaliser denied us. It's a pity.

I look back at my career, and we got to the All-Ireland final in my first four years and again the last year, and you're looking at the part in between and thinking we did nothing for such a big county and the calibre of player that was there.

At the same time, a once-in-a-generation Kilkenny team came along and won all around them. You'd love to know what would have happened if Cork had won the All-Ireland in 2006 – what way we'd have gone and what way Kilkenny would have gone.

Kilkenny might have continued to improve and win all of those other All-Irelands, but it's an interesting 'sliding doors' moment.

It would have been nice to have won more but, to be fair, I wouldn't have many regrets from my playing days. Something that the late, great Eamonn Ryan said was that he always dreamed of playing with Cork, but he didn't dream of winning with Cork.

I think every youngster is like that.

Coming from a small parish and then on up through the ranks, with Farranferris and UCC and then on to Cork, I feel honoured and privileged to have done all of that.

99

SHANE O'NEILL
(& BEN O'CONNOR)

CORK 0-23   GALWAY 2-15
All-Ireland SHC Qualifier Round 4
Semple Stadium
JULY 19, 2008

Shane O'Neill takes the ball away against Galway in 2008, with Joe Canning in pursuit.

★ **CORK:** D Óg Cusack; **S O'Neill**, D O'Sullivan, B Murphy; J Gardiner (0-2), R Curran, S Óg Ó hAilpín; T Kenny, J O'Connor; P Cronin, N McCarthy (0-1), T McCarthy; **B O'Connor (0-12)**, J Deane (0-4), C Naughton (0-3). Subs: P Horgan (0-1) for T McCarthy, M Coleman for Naughton, Naughton for O'Sullivan.

★ **TEAM:** J Skehill; D Joyce, A Cullinane, O Canning; S Kavanagh, J Lee, D Forde; F Healy, R Murray (0-1); K Hayes, I Tannion, A Kerins; D Hayes (0-1), J Canning (2-12), N Healy (0-1). Subs: C Dervan for Joyce, A Smith for K Hayes, A Callanan for Kerins, G Farragher for Hayes, C Donnellan for F Healy.

THE ACTION

GALWAY HAD BEATEN Antrim by 6-21 to 1-10 and Laois by 1-26 to 0-9, but this was Joe Canning's first 'real' championship game. He would finish with 2-12 and the Man of the Match award, but incredibly, that wasn't enough for the Tribesmen in what proved to be Ger Loughnane's last match in charge.

The Rebels, who had been knocked out of the Munster Championship by Tipperary before seeing off Dublin unconvincingly in their first qualifier, had the game's first four points but then Canning announced himself to the wider hurling world with an excellent goal. They were soon level and while John Gardiner put Cork 0-8 to 1-4 ahead, the game was about to turn. A Galway attack looked to have ended with Alan Kerins netting, but referee Barry Kelly had blown his whistle a second earlier for a foul by Dónal Óg Cusack and, with the goalkeeper already booked, he was dismissed. Replacement Martin Coleman couldn't do anything to keep out Canning's drilled penalty and, after Canning and Ben O'Connor swapped frees, Galway led by 2-5 to 0-9 at half-time.

In the confusion after Cusack's sending-off, it was Cathal Naughton who was called ashore to allow Coleman to come on, but Naughton was back on the field for the second-half, with Diarmuid O'Sullivan off and Gardiner now operating at full-back. Canning's brother Ollie looked to be the perfect choice as Galway's spare man but they couldn't pull more than three points clear and Cork began to sense that the game was there for them if they wanted it.

Six successive points were reeled off by the men in red, with Joe Deane, O'Connor and Naughton all among the scorers, and sub Patrick Horgan was unlucky to be denied a goal by James Skehill. Ben O'Connor's tenth point of the day made it 0-18 to 2-9 for Cork, as the Galway wides tally clicked to 13. Cork pushed five clear but Galway refused to throw in the towel. Niall Healy and Richie Murray both pointed, the latter going for goal, while Canning got three late points, but it was Cork's day.

O'Connor had the final say to leave him with 12 at the end and the pitch invasion showed what the win meant to the Cork fans.

★★★★★

66

THE FIRST CORK game I went to in Croke Park was the 1992 All-Ireland final against Kilkenny and the first one I remember going to in Páirc Uí Chaoimh was in '96 – Jimmy Barry-Murphy's first year – when they were beaten by Limerick in the pouring rain.

When I was brought on to the panel in 2005, I was still a Cork supporter and I had been to all the games that year as a fan, either on the terraces with the lads or in the stand with my family. I was absolutely overawed... by whom I was sitting next to in the dressing-room or what these guys were like off the field.

I was trying to learn and take in as much as I could, without trying to burn the ear off them either.

That day in Thurles in 2008 against Galway – even though I was part of the team and playing for the 70 minutes – once the final whistle blew and we won, it was like I was a fan again. That day, I ripped my helmet off and started running up the field.

I wasn't a player at that moment, it was like I was invading the pitch with the rest of the supporters. It was sheer delight that Cork won a game, one that nobody gave us a chance of winning.

I can never pinpoint a specific time or something that happened, where a switch went off in my brain and I said... *Jesus, I can make it.*

Definitely, there was no one moment – it was always a dream or an aspiration when I was growing up that I wanted to play with Cork, but I would say that one hundred percent of kids growing up in the county playing hurling and football for their clubs have the same kind of goal.

As I progressed through the underage system with Cork, it became more of a possibility. I played two years Cork minor and that was a big thing – you're playing before the seniors and there's a bit of a crowd... we won a Munster final, that kind of thing. That was my first big step in terms of higher-pressure games and, I suppose, I was fortunate that it happened naturally enough after that. I graduated to under-21, played Fitzgibbon for a few years... and it all happened in such a short space of time.

The Bishopstown team that I played on won the under-15 county, the under-16 county… we won two minors in-a-row, two under-21s in-a-row.

In a five- or six-year period we barely lost a game and, at the same time as the under-21 wins, we won the Premier Intermediate Championship to go up senior. So, there was a huge amount done with Bishopstown in a short period, in parallel to my own progress with Cork and UCC.

People from the club often ask me what we had or what we created, but there were definitely a few things. Luck played a part in that there were 25 or 30 young kids of that age that started playing in Bishopstown that year.

We were also a really close-knit group; we were all best friends and it was never a situation where we would only see each other once or twice a week at training. At under-12, say, training might have been on a Wednesday and a Saturday, but we were all up in 'the Gah' pucking around every other day.

For whatever reason, that's what we did – when we were hanging around, we all had our hurleys. We were all close friends and we loved it.

And the coaching we got in Bishopstown really benefited us. The only manager that I had from the age of six or seven up to when we won intermediate was a guy called Pádraig O'Donoghue and it was more or less a one-man show. He took no nonsense and he gave it to us between the eyes, to be honest.

That kind of management or coaching isn't really done anymore.

I'm not saying I disagree with how kids are coached nowadays but it would have been more old school. You would have been given out to and you would have been disciplined but, not only did it stand to us on the pitch, it stood to us in life.

I think we all learned a lot from the way he disciplined us – treat your friends with respect, treat your coaches with respect, respect the opposition… and then train and work hard. Those were the principles that we had from a very young age.

Ciarán McGann and myself were called on to the Cork senior panel either the week before or the week of the 2005 All-Ireland semi-final against Clare. I was lucky enough to be playing with UCC at the time and so were Tom Kenny and Kevin Hartnett, who would have been on the Cork panel for a while.

I can remember them saying that it would take a while for your body to adapt to it. I was used to playing and training at a minor or under-21 level and not going to the gym once or twice a week, so obviously Cork senior training was a massive step up in terms of fitness, preparation and skill.

It took me a while to adjust to the rigours of training. I was relatively small – I'm 5ft 11in – and I was slight enough, maybe 75kg or 80kg, so I needed to put on a bit of mass, as well.

I don't think I ever modelled my game on anyone but I would have looked up massively to Brian Corcoran and Wayne Sherlock. They were two top class defenders and absolute gents off the field as well.

And when I went in, in 2005, there was Wayne Sherlock and there was Brian Corcoran, and I still looked up to them massively.

Cork retained the All-Ireland that year and I received a medal – I couldn't tell you where it is, though. I can remember one of my friends saying at the time that it might mean a lot to me in the future and, I suppose, you think that Cork will always be there and always be competing.

I did get another chance to win a medal, in 2013, but obviously not as many opportunities as I would have liked.

Does the 2005 medal mean much?

Maybe, looking back on my career now, I can say that I have one but it's not the same and I was only on the panel for a few weeks beforehand. As a career thing, it counts for something but, as a stand-alone All-Ireland in 2005, I had absolutely nothing to do with Cork achieving it.

For the end of 2005, '06 and the vast majority of '07, it was about learning my trade and training hard, just getting used to the rigours of it.

I played centre-back at under-age level but I played corner-back and wing-back for the Cork minors as well. If I got a run for the last 10 minutes of a league game or challenge match for the seniors, I was probably always coming on at corner-back.

When you look at the half-back line, with Ronan Curran, John Gardiner and Seán Óg Ó hAilpín there at that time, there wasn't really a chance of anyone breaking in there! In terms of physicality and size, I was definitely more suited to the corner.

I did play half-back a bit for my club, but the full-back line is very different. You're not on the ball as much and you're not striking it as much, and you're way more concerned about being tight with your man and where he is, trying to judge where the ball is going to go next. My hurling and my skill level definitely dipped a bit when I was in the full-back line – it's a different game, you're not going to be delivering ball into the full-forwards. Your skill-set there compared to midfield or wing-back is very different.

How I initially got my chance was after Semplegate – Dónal Óg Cusack, Diarmuid O'Sullivan and Seán Óg Ó hAilpín were all suspended after the Munster quarter-final win over Clare in 2007. I knew I had a chance of being picked for the semi-final against Waterford – you have to think like that when you're a sub anyway, you're not just there to make up the numbers and you want to be pushing for a starting position.

When you get your chance at that level, you have to take it.

You see it in a lot of sports – if things don't go well on that day, you mightn't get a second chance.

Anthony Nash made his debut in goal and Kevin Hartnett was in at wing-back for Seán Óg – he had come on against Clare, but it was his first start. Cian O'Connor was full-back, after being corner-back against Clare. He's a few years older than me and he played a bit in the league and in the 2006 championship, but it was still a fairly new defence... the four of us alongside Brian Murphy, 'Gaa' and Curran.

When you're younger, it's probably a bit easier to play with freedom and you tend to not over-think things, whether it's your preparations coming up to a game, or the day of the match. I definitely remember, for the first few years with Cork, I probably wasn't thinking... *I need to mind myself here!* Or that I needed to get certain things absolutely perfect in terms of preparation for a game.

With experience, you take a step back and realise that you do need to mind yourself and do X, Y and Z to prepare well. But obviously there's a balance, because if you do too much of that, you're over-thinking it and wasting energy.

That day against Waterford, I never really thought about our inexperience but if you were part of the Waterford forward line, you'd have been thinking... *We could go to town on these guys!* I was marking Paul Flynn that day.

Cork had developed a great rivalry with Waterford around that time and they were always unbelievable games... high-scoring, free-flowing, little or no tactics and there were goals and points flying in all over the place.

Obviously, Flynn was in the thick of it – he was the one getting the goals and points, and then I found myself marking him and thinking... *Jesus Christ, this is serious stuff.*

It's amazing how quickly the game goes.

There's such a build-up to a championship game, so much hype around it, everybody's talking about it – and it's only 70 minutes. It literally just by-passes you.

Even with Bishopstown, I would have been more nervous coming up to the game and just before it. But I was always more relaxed when the game started – once the whistle goes and the ball is thrown in, it was like... *The game is on now and it's time to get to work.*

Looking back at my debut game that day, I can remember just before the game and just after it but, as for the game itself, I can't remember a whole pile. Which is probably a good thing to be able to say as a corner back!

We lost by three points but we all played well – I don't know what the bookies' odds were but I'd say most people thought that Waterford would beat us handy enough. There were plenty of positives to take from that game.

I kept my place for the next nine or 10 seasons. Obviously, my form dipped at times throughout my career but that was natural as well.

I was in UCC at the time of being called up to the senior panel, but I never felt like my GAA involvement was denying me the extra-curricular college experience. It helped that I had a lot of close friends from Bishopstown in the same boat.

Obviously, Pa Cronin was playing with Cork too and Ken O'Halloran was with the footballers. I'd be very good friends with Michael Shields and he was with the footballers... and Fintan Goold was in the same class as me in UCC. Don't get me wrong, we had our nights out too, but maybe not to the same extent as the average student.

If I didn't have lads making the same sacrifices as me, it would have been a lot harder.

We could talk about the strikes and that winter and that pre-season for hours. A lot of the senior members of the panel had way more riding on the 2007-08 strike than myself and the younger fellas. I had the Fitzgibbon, which was a valuable outlet for me, but they weren't good times at all.

It was all over the media and the rumour-mill was going ninety.

It was awful, really.

We stayed training, but obviously not to the same levels or standards that other senior inter county teams were training to at that time. And, we weren't as well organised because we hadn't any backroom team in place with us.

There was a decent amount of us that were attending UCC and CIT at that time so that helped keep our skill-levels up. When we did get back on the field – after Cork had to give walkovers in the first two league games – there was a sense that we had to crack on to make up for the lost time.

The way we started against Tipp, it looked like we might do that but they came back strongly and beat us. The back door had been there a while so, even though you were disappointed to lose a big Munster Championship match, you were thinking of the qualifiers straightaway. There's no point feeling sorry for yourself – you had another chance coming in a few weeks and you needed to get back on the horse very quickly.

From then on, it is proper championship and do-or-die stuff.

We had Dublin first at home and we didn't play well that day at all; it was a poor performance but we won and we were still in the championship. It's a cliché but if you can get a run in the qualifiers, you build up momentum as the games come thick and fast.

I was never massively superstitious.

I would have tried to get my nutrition and hydration correct, and get as much sleep and rest as I could but, if anything, I tried to take my mind off the game. I might go to the cinema with the lads on the Friday or Saturday night – I wouldn't have been locking myself away or anything.

From a young age, I wore my socks up and even up to the last few years with Bishopstown, it was something I did – nowadays, most guys can't do it as they wear those fancy ankle socks. I think it was just an old-school thing. Similarly, I always had a black helmet and would have favoured black grips and black tape on my hurley.

The tradition for games in Thurles was that we'd go to the Anner Hotel after games, and beforehand we'd go to Dundrum House Hotel. It was quieter and a bit out of the way.

We hadn't been playing particularly well, there was the strike stuff simmering in the background and there was a plenty of talk around Galway with Ger

Loughnane in charge, so nobody really gave us a chance.

Personally, that was a situation I loved because it felt like a free shot.

In effect, we had nothing to lose. You'd be a bit annoyed at being written off, with all the… *This is Galway's game to lose* kind of thing. That was in the back of all of our minds.

When Dónal Óg was sent off, I presume most people thought that would be *that*.

Unless we were playing a game of backs and forwards or taking shots on the keepers, they trained by themselves. Even before I was on the panel, when I used to go along to watch sessions as a kid, the keepers were always nearly the most interesting fellas to watch – their skill levels were off the charts.

So, when Cusack was sent off that day, there was never any doubt, whether it was Martin Coleman or Nash coming in, about them doing a job because we knew they all trained together and were able to fill in.

It was more… *F**k, we're down to 14 men and nobody's giving us a chance.*

There is that moment when the doubts creep in, so we just needed to get in at half-time and come up with a plan. It was calm inside – there were no hurleys hopping off the ground or people blaming anyone or anything like that.

Cusack spoke to the team before we went out and there was this feeling that we were still in the game, still fighting. There was definitely a feeling among the team when we were leaving the dressing-room that we were going to win the game.

Cathal Naughton had started but he was the player brought off for Marty, when Cusack was sent off. Then he was brought back on at half-time and there was one point he got in the second-half, I can't remember if it was to level or put us ahead, but it sticks out.

Obviously, he was an absolute rocket when it came to running with the ball and he was going down the left wing in loads of space, and put it over. He was running back the field, probably at the same pace as he had been with the ball, and he threw his arms up to the crowd and I just remember the roar and the sound and thinking… *We have Galway rattled and the crowd behind us.*

Everything seemed to flow after that.

A lot of my friends from Bishopstown had gone away to America on J1s that summer but there were two buddies – 'Bullets' and Ollies – still around so I gave them my ticket allocation for most of the games that year.

I met them on the pitch after the game and it was magic – definitely the best feeling I've ever had after any game.

Certainly, the memories from the win that day mean a lot more to me than my All-Ireland medal.

BEN O'CONNOR

The euphoria that followed the final whistle and the defeat of Galway with 14 men in 2008 has never been forgotten by Ben O'Connor.

"

THAT DAY AGAINST Galway – and it doesn't happen too often – every fella came up trumps.

I've won All-Irelands and bits and pieces here and there, but even then, it mightn't happen – in my whole hurling career, it might have only happened three times.

But, when it was needed that night, that's what happened.

You couldn't beat Thurles, going up there on a Sunday for a championship match.

Now, that was a Saturday evening but heading off for Thurles is a day out for everyone. We used to always meet the bus in Mitchelstown – it would have been way shorter to head over to Tipperary town, and on that way, and meet the boys in Dundrum but, when I started with Jimmy in 1999, before the first championship match, he said, 'We'll meet you in Mitchelstown so!'

I said that was perfect. I was delighted to be heading off over to Mitchelstown, I didn't care which was the longest way or the shortest way, and I just found then that going to Mitchelstown was all part of the trip.

You'd have to be going off early because, with the crowds going to the matches and no motorway, there'd be huge tail-backs going into Mitchelstown. Even if you were only 10 minutes behind time, the bus would be waiting for you and you wouldn't want that happening!

Even out on the field, I'd probably prefer Thurles to Croke Park.

With the atmosphere and everything, it's just a day out.

At the time, not that you'd even be thinking about it, we had a lot of bad press and people were saying that we were finished.

We had been beaten by Tipperary in Páirc Uí Chaoimh and there was a bit of pressure on, but it wasn't ourselves putting on that pressure, it was from outside… *These lads are done.*

The thing is that the older fellas weren't that old, either, but there was a lot of mileage on the clock.

I remember coming up to that game, and even for the games before it, there was stick. I had a piece that somebody had posted, a report in some paper down around West Cork and it was just abusing fellas.

I was mentioned in it because I had said in an interview a few weeks beforehand that I didn't care what the public thought – which I didn't, all I was worried about was what was inside in the group. And obviously some fella down there picked up from it that I was arrogant… and I was this and I was that.

The way I looked at it, was that I was meeting up with these fellas four or five nights a week for nine months and this fella was standing outside and he was abusing me and my buddies. I felt that I was sticking up for them.

Anyway, some fella sent this to me to drive me on, I suppose, so I had that in my bag all year long.

The problem in the wake of the strike was that it was split, you'd fifty percent for us and fifty percent against us. For every fella that said something like that, there was someone else outside backing us to the hilt as well.

If we were beaten that night, it was the end of a lot of fellas.

Being last on the bus meant that you couldn't choose your seat, so it was just a case of sitting wherever the boys would let you. Some fellas wouldn't want anyone sitting with them, so you'd just walk down and you'd see a fella shuffling and sit in with him.

Sometimes, fellas would have a bag outside them or a box to keep you away, so you just knew. It was wherever you got a seat.

In every dressing-room I went into, I had my spot and I always had to be within two or three seats of that. Alongside me, I'd have Ronan Curran on one side and Brian Murphy on the other. That's the way it was, we'd always sit together and most fellas were the same.

They'd have a place they'd go that they were used to.

We used to talk away.

You'd see some fellas inside there with their earphones on and Curran would be like that after a while; he'd listen to a bit of music, but there was always a bit of craic going on. The way we hurled, if fellas were relaxed, they'd hurl away mad, but if you were uptight, you couldn't. We had no fellas that were *not* talkers, really.

Some would go in and out to the field before the match to see what it was like – whether it was greasy or if the grass was long – but I never used to.

Even after we went out, I wouldn't overdo it with practising frees.

If I hit the first one over the bar then that was the end of it, but if I missed the first, second, third, I'd keep hitting them until I got one.

Once I'd one hit over the bar, that was it.

No more practising, let it happen then if it was going to happen. It was about trusting the routine – I'd be afraid to be wasting the good ones!

If I put too many over the bar, they were ones that you might miss during the game… so stop using them up after that.

I haven't a notion as to who was marking me – I don't even know did I play on the wing or in the corner… probably on the wing.

Dónal Óg Cusack getting the road was harsh, really – he gave a fella a little bit of a tap and there were a few words said earlier on.

That night, I thought Cusack got his two yellows for who he was, rather than what he had done. If it was any other goalkeeper, he'd have got a warning or there'd have been something said… to be sent off for what he did was scandalous.

You wouldn't even get sent off for that today and things have changed a lot since then.

Cusack was sent off after, what, 22 or 23 minutes?

He was gone and that's when the real pressure was on. At the same time, Martin Coleman slotted in seamlessly. The reason for that was that our goalkeepers were so well-prepared, it made no difference.

Cusack was in goal nearly all the time that I played, but Anthony Nash and Martin were there too and they knew exactly what was happening. If one of them had to be fired in, they knew exactly what was going on and nothing changed; they all had the same puckout tactic and so on.

That just shows the importance of small details – you have 15 players, but every sub on the panel has to be tuned in. In fairness, that night Martin was.

Then, not only that, but to lose Diarmuid O'Sullivan. Now, he was having his hands full that night with Joe Canning, who was on fire. Cathal Naughton had to be taken off to let on Martin Coleman, but the decision was made to bring him in again at half-time.

Sully had to go off and John Gardiner went in full-back, a place where he didn't want to play or didn't like to play, but just for the 35 minutes or so that was in it, he went back there and did the business.

We went in at half-time and there was no roaring or shouting, no jumping around the place, everything was calm. There was just a chat inside and every fella said… *This is it, we're either going to die here, fighting to win this, or else we can call our inter-county careers over.* That's what it was, every fella knew his job.

Everything was explained out as to what had to be done and every fella carried it out to a tee.

I just think we were so focused, especially after Cusack went off, because he had a lot done for a lot of fellas. We wanted to make sure that it wasn't going to be the way that he was going to go out.

Obviously, you need the bit of luck as well but every fella was just so tuned in and knew exactly what they were doing. Sometimes you see it, that a team gets a fella sent off and it rises everyone else. That's all we needed.

Galway went in leading by four points at half-time and I'm nearly sure that we were turning around against the breeze in the second-half, into the Town End, but that suited us.

You might say how would that suit us, playing with 14 men into the wind, but the ball was going shorter, it was dropping in front of fellas and guys out the field knew that they weren't going to score from 70 yards.

Instead of taking the pot-shot, they were dropping it in low, into the fellas running the wings and running the corners.

Fifteen against 15, I always like to turn around for the second-half and have the breeze at our backs. It was just the way that, on that night with 14 against 15, it suited.

As well as that, Galway had a few wides because they had fellas shooting from way out the field with the breeze. Our fellas weren't wasting balls like that, they knew that every one was so important, they had to find one of our guys and, if they didn't, they were going to be under pressure out the field again.

The other side of it is that, on that team, you'd legs all over the place.

You'd fellas who could cover ground, and fellas that would hook and block and wouldn't give up. It made a huge difference. It was going to be *legs* that were going to win it. With the way Galway played, they never pushed forward, they kept the extra fella back all the time. They had one of their corner-backs free but he stood inside, where he wasn't affecting the game.

After Cusack was sent off, word was sent in to us, 'Play down the sides, play down the sides!' Every fella knew then where to put the ball to keep the spare man out of play.

Everything just clicked, every plan and every idea that we went to. You knew that you could turn around and the fella alongside you was giving everything.

I remember with about two minutes to go, we were defending, up a point or two, and a ball broke into our corner-back position.

I was back there and I went to go for it.

I made a burst for it and I got a cramp – and very few times did I cramp up during a match. I still tried to go for it and, next thing, this fella shot by me and said, 'I'll get there, I'll get there!'

It was Curran. He saw that I was after getting cramp and he got there.

Myself and Cathal Naughton were over by the sideline when the whistle went and the crowd that came on to the field – I've never experienced anything like it in my life. The feeling was amazing.

It took us ages to get in off the field; it was great to be outside but I just wanted to get in to the boys. When we got in, I met Dr Con and our physio Declan O'Sullivan – I've seen them happy after matches before but I've never seen them as happy as they were that night.

And that's the same for a lot of the fellas I played with – I've never seen fellas celebrate a qualifier as much in all my life.

It was like an All-Ireland final.

I don't believe I felt like that after any other match I ever played.

We went to the Anner Hoel for our dinner, walking away down the town and, because we were playing Clare the following weekend, there were no pints… so we all got an ice-cream. I got home at half past 11 or midnight and I slept no wink that night, I suppose it was adrenaline… I saw every hour of the clock and I'd the television on all night.

We trained again on the Monday night and we were talking about it and nearly every fella was the same. No fella slept because they were all so pumped up.

It's just one of those things that you can't explain, just the feeling.

We played in bigger matches but I don't think I've ever got as much joy out of anything as we did that night.

STEPHEN McDONNELL

CORK 2-23   CLARE 2-18
Munster SHC Semi-Final
Semple Stadium
JUNE 15, 2014

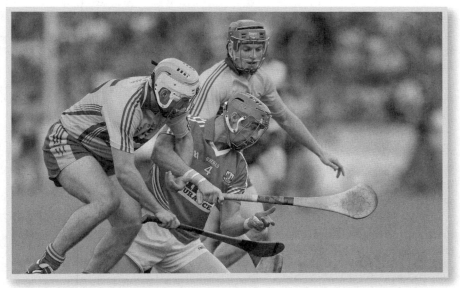

Stephen McDonnell sees only the ball against Clare in the Munster Championship in 2014.

★ **CORK:** A Nash; S O'Neill, **S McDonnell**, C Joyce; D Cahalane (0-1), M Ellis, L McLoughlin; D Kearney (0-3), A Walsh (0-1); S Harnedy, B Cooper, C Lehane (0-2); A Cadogan (0-3), P Horgan (2-11), P Cronin. Subs: S Moylan for Cooper, W Egan (0-1) for Kearney, P O'Sullivan (0-1) for Harnedy, E Cadogan for Ellis.

★ **CLARE:** D Tuohy; D McInerney, C Dillon, J Browne; P O'Connor, Conor Ryan, B Bugler; C Galvin (0-2), P Donnellan (0-1); J Conlon (1-2), Colin Ryan (0-6), P Duggan; T Kelly (0-1), C McGrath (0-2), P Collins (0-1). Subs: S Morey for Browne, N O'Connell (0-2) for Donnellan, C McInerney (0-1) for Galvin, D Honan (1-0) for Conlon.

THE ACTION

IN 2013, CORK reached the All-Ireland final for the first time in eight years and were seconds away from winning the Liam MacCarthy Cup for the 31st time, until Clare corner-back Domhnall O'Donovan scored a dramatic late equaliser. The Banner were the better side in the replay, winning by 5-16 to 3-16.

With Clare having also won the All-Ireland under-21 title that year, they were backed to progress the following season, while Cork faced question-marks. The doubts about the Rebels increased as they scraped a draw with Waterford in the Munster quarter-final, but an impressive replay win saw them set up a re-match with Clare.

The sides were level on six occasions in the first-half before Cork began to make use of the wind at their backs, and Jimmy Barry-Murphy's team were 0-12 to 0-10 ahead as half-time approached.

When they were awarded a free just outside the 20-metre line, Patrick Horgan – who had already scored eight points – went for goal and was duly rewarded. However, Clare struck back almost immediately, as John Conlon goaled for them.

Midfielders Daniel Kearney and Aidan Walsh combined effectively to ensure that Cork stayed in front through the second-half and the lead was 1-20 to 1-16, when Séamus Harnedy was fouled for a penalty, which Horgan drilled past Donal Tuohy in the Clare goal.

Clare sub Darach Honan did find the net for them at the very end, but the goal only served to slightly redress the imbalance on the scoreboard as Cork advanced to a Munster final meeting with Limerick for the second successive year.

★★★★★

"

I CAPTAINED CORK to win a Munster Championship in 2017 and we were massive underdogs that year, so it's hard for me to look beyond that.

I also had another really memorable game in the 2013 All-Ireland final replay, where I got nominated for Man of the Match, but we lost, so the 2014 Munster semi-final against Clare was one of the best games I've played… and we beat the All-Ireland champions from the year before.

So that's the game that edges it.

In 2010, when Denis Walsh was the Cork senior manager, they were going to a training camp in Waterford. They wanted to play a 15-on-15 game but they didn't have the numbers, so they got on to myself and Luke O'Farrell, and a taxi driver collected us by the church near the train station in Cork and brought us to Waterford to play the game… and brought us back down again!

That was my first taste of the senior team, and they brought me in properly then in 2011 and I played championship that year. The first championship match was Tipperary in Thurles and I was put marking Lar Corbett, who had won Hurler of the Year in 2010… so it was great craic!

I enjoyed that, though – I always loved pressure.

Here's the best fella on the team, you have to take him out of the game.

I was a regular starter from then on.

There was one period in 2012, where we lost the league final and I had a bad game – there were one or two balls I made a mistake for – and Jimmy took me out for one of the championship games, but otherwise I was starting, with the exception of my final season where I was carrying an injury and in the deep end of fatherhood.

But even at that, I still felt that I was the best man to do a job on anyone and in the games I played, I got the better of my man!

You definitely can be a man-marker and play a proactive game.

Obviously, I need to keep an eye on them but I can dictate by positioning myself so that they've only one way to go, or I always have them thinking on their feet. I know what they want to do… so I'm looking to stop that. The closer they are to the end-line, the more room they have to come to the ball or make a move, so I'll pull them out past the 20-metre line.

I always have them thinking, I always have them under pressure, forcing my game on them. It's about not letting up, having a hand on them, a pull or a drag – knowing what position they want to be in and pushing them to one where they don't want to be.

I'd be proactive in that sense but then, as a defender, if a ball is coming in and they have space outside, it can be hard. If you know he's going to get the ball, you have to leave him get it and use your speed, or stand them up and do the right thing.

Sometimes, you have to concede a point to make sure it's not a goal, and you just take that as it comes and react. You might see a back drop his head after his man gets a point but you just have to get on with it, because there's no room for dwelling on things… and the next ball can come in straightaway.

If you're not present in the moment, it can be a goal, so you have to get over things very quickly.

I was captain of the Cork minors in 2007 as the Glen had won the minor county in '06 but I was dropped after the Munster final against Tipperary. It was a difficult one for me, to be honest.

I was doing shift-work that summer, working nights in GE Healthcare in Carrigtwohill. The lads used to collect me in the morning after I finished my shift and I'd go straight to training. I was trying to play minor for Cork and senior with the Glen, as well as all the work… I was exhausted.

As a young fella, you're not as mature and it does take longer to deal with setbacks but, if you do deal with them, you do come back stronger. I felt that, obviously, I was exhausted physically and that affects you mentally – you're not going to be as quick off the mark or sharp enough.

You're dealing with all of that and you have the pressure of being captain on your shoulders, representing the Glen and your family. I'd all of that there as a negative force, so there was a lot pulling me back.

Tim Gallwey has written a lot of books about coaching and what he calls 'the inner game' – he has a formula, that potential minus resistance or interference equals performance. I had huge potential but I had massive interference and that affected my performance.

I have a business now where I support leaders and teams around the world activate this unrealised potential. Coming out of minor, I was offered Cork under-21 trials, as I was going well with the Glen, but I didn't want to play for Cork for a year or two after that.

I started for the under-21s in 2010 and Tipperary beat us in a great game down in Páirc Uí Chaoimh… Séamus Hennessy buried a goal in the last minute of extra-time to win it for them. They were an exceptional team and many of them went on to carry Tipp at senior level for the last decade.

In terms of players I would have looked to emulate growing up, Derek Lyng from Kilkenny is one. I know he was a midfielder but I felt that he always worked very hard for the team and had a strong presence out there.

I liked Wayne Sherlock as well, I thought he was a very smart hurler, and Brian Murphy was also a very good role model. He was very good at going in there and doing a job.

Jimmy Barry-Murphy was a great manager, Kieran Kingston also and he showed huge belief in me by giving me the captain's role. And Ian Lynam in the Glen had a big influence on my career. We won the Féile at under-14 level with him as selector/coach and he stayed with us the whole way up – we won the under-14 county, under-16 county, two minors and under-21. He was coach then when we won the senior county, so I won a championship with him at every level.

He's a very good tactical coach and a man of few words, but he spoke very well and made you believe in yourself. It's a huge thing for me, if you have a manager that believes in you and trusts you to do a hard job.

I used to get a lot of confidence from guys giving me the job of marking the opposition's best player – and all of the best managers I was under had that belief in me.

We made it to the All-Ireland final in 2013 and drew with Clare.

I was on Podge Collins and didn't play very well – I was average, really.

Podge did a few good things and I was pissed off and it was my own fault: I didn't deal with the pressure well and I had to manage that better the next day.

I looked at what was holding me back the most and it was my mindset and my belief in myself. so I worked on that between the two matches. Basically, it was about being more positive, having better internal dialogue and showing more courage.

I knew that I had to just shut everything else out and play the game and drive the team on – I wasn't going to wait for anyone else to do it.

I was going to do it.

Tony Kelly had done a lot of damage in the first game, so I was put out centre-back to try to limit him and I got on a world of ball.

I was hurling away and I got the better of him; I was giving everything I could, I was completely in the moment in the game and before I knew it, it was over. I was nominated for Man of the Match – two Clare players and myself – so that was nice recognition to have, something to look back on with pride, even though we lost.

I gave my all and I knew I helped the team whatever way I could.

I was proud of that.

There were three weeks between the drawn match and the replay, so that was a challenging time, but an exciting time. They beat us comprehensively, to be fair, and they had been the better team the first day.

We knew we were underdogs so everything had to go right, we needed to all play well and there was no room for error. Their forwards were really good that year, they were capable of putting up high scores, and we defended fairly openly.

When we lost, it wasn't a major shock but it took a lot of energy out of us because All-Ireland finals are hard – wonderful, but hard.

Two finals in the space of three weeks took a massive effort, so there's a part of you relieved that you're out the other side of it, but the disappointment sets in more as the time goes on. As the weeks went by, you realised that the opportunity had gone and you'd lost… and you were wondering if you'd get the chance again.

It's more of a longer, sustained disappointment and you carry that into the following year.

Clare won the under-21 All-Ireland in 2013 too, and they were being tipped to push on and win more, whereas Cork were seen as having missed a chance and were being written off. You try to ignore all of that talk but it's hard; fellas hear it in their own clubs and that was another factor that was there as well.

Tom Kenny and Seán Óg Ó Hailpín had retired, and it was being said that we were in transition… it would be three or four years before we'd get there again and all of that kind of stuff. You do have all of that, so first of all you need to manage it internally yourself and then walk through it as a team, too.

The more elephants in the room you have, the more weight there is and that was an elephant in the room for a few years.

In some ways, it took until 2017 to get over it and that was a great year – obviously, I was captain, so it was special from a personal point of view.

The year before that, 2016, had been an awful year. We lost to Wexford in the qualifiers and I broke my elbow in a challenge match against Clare after an off-the-ball incident. So, to come back from that and be given the opportunity as captain in 2017 and win Munster against all odds – beating Tipp, Waterford and Clare after being ranked fifth in Munster at the start of the year – was brilliant.

We won it by being a strong, cohesive, hard-working, honest team.

Our first game in 2014 was a Munster quarter-final against Waterford and we were bad that day, lucky to get a draw. We were probably listening to the talk around the place. The result gave us a bit of a kick... *We can go through this year willy-nilly, just hoping for the best and that kind of stuff... or we can do something about it.* We knew we all had to drive it on and, to be fair, we did – we came back and beat Waterford and that set us up well for the semi-final against Clare.

We had actually played Clare five times in 2013 – the two All-Ireland finals, obviously, and there was a Waterford Crystal Cup pre-season game in Sixmilebridge, as well as the league relegation play-off and the Munster Championship match, both of which were in Limerick. The 2014 match was set for Thurles and there's a different energy there.

Even as a young fella, it was special – with no disrespect intended, you don't travel to the Gaelic Grounds for the Munster Championship... it's all about Thurles. When I went to games as a supporter, we used to get a bus from the church in Ballyvolane up to Thurles.

As a player, when you're going through Liberty Square on the bus to a match, you're bringing all of those memories back and there's a different vibe.

We buzzed off that and Cork teams have always enjoyed going into that environment. It brought a little bit more pressure and we fed off it – you can either rise up or sink down in those situations... and we rose up.

I used to keep things very simple in the lead-up.

The closer I'd get to a big game, the more time I'd spend alone.

I'd try to block out the talk around the match and just focus inwardly and get myself ready. I'd eat healthy and train well, obviously, but then I'd put the hurley away. Something else I used to do was go to the beach, a day or two days beforehand.

If it was the day before, it'd be Fountainstown or Ballybrannigan, as they're only a half-hour away. If it was two or three days before, I'd go to Inchydoney for a walk on the beach and a bit of stretching, before going to the sauna and steam room and a swim in the pool.

The other thing – from about 2017 onwards, as I became more experienced – was not to bring a phone as I didn't want to be looking through dozens of messages on the day of a match. I left my proper phone at home and got an old non-smartphone, for which only my girlfriend Erika had the number.

I see some fellas in the dressing-room before a game and they'd be on social media, flicking through stuff – I don't know how they do it!

Some lads would go out to the pitch for a look and maybe sit down and watch the first game, but I'd go out, take one quick look around and go back in.

I'd usually be in the dressing-room on my own for about five minutes.

I broke my hand in 2012 and I should have got an operation but I didn't, as I'd have been out for longer, and it didn't heal properly; the middle finger on my left hand just hangs out.

It takes eight or nine minutes to go through the process of taping the hand up.

For 2014, I was put marking Conor McGrath, who had done the most damage of any forward in the All-Ireland final. He got a goal and, any time he got the ball, it would bring a roar of anticipation from the crowd.

I was put on him to do a job, so I was delighted with that.

I had an idea it might happen but I usually wouldn't find out until the last session before the match – I'd go over to the management after training and ask what the plan was for the full-back, but I didn't do that for the Clare game.

I knew they were thinking on it and there were a few different forwards to plan for.

It wasn't until we stopped off at Dundrum on the way up that Kieran Kingston – who was coach at the time – brought me into one of the rooms and said, 'You're going to pick up McGrath and he's not going to touch a ball!' Basically, that was the instruction – the pressure was on, but I was delighted with it.

It gave me focus, gave me a target and I went out and absolutely cleaned him out – he might have got a point or two, but I was on the most possessions for the game.

There was ball after ball going into him, but I was getting on it all the time. In the first minute, Conor Ryan sent a ball towards us and I gave McGrath a shove so that it would go over his head and behind.

It was a foot-race then, which I won; I got the ball and cleared it, and Aidan Walsh plucked it out of the sky. There was a huge cheer and Jimmy said it to me afterwards, that it gave everyone a lift. After that, we started to take over.

It was nice to win the first ball but you wouldn't place too much significance on it, either – sometimes, the attacker might win it and do something with it and you just had to accept that things like that happen.

I never let that get the better of me – you wouldn't last long in the full-back line if it was bothering you.

We were always that bit better than Clare on the day and it was a great one for us to win. Clare had beaten us over the two games in 2013, so you'd question the ability of the team and how you stack up against the All-Ireland champions is how you measure how good you are. When we beat them, it reiterated that we were on the right track and we needed to keep going. After beating the All-Ireland champions, we were very confident going into the Limerick game.

When I look back on my career, could we have won an All-Ireland?

We could.

The team in 2017 was probably the best collective that I was part of with Cork, but we had a man sent off in the All-Ireland semi-final against Waterford and didn't react well to that, eventually losing the game.

It's tough, but I can reflect back on my career and say that I did everything I could and there's a satisfaction in that.

ANTHONY NASH

CORK 2-24   LIMERICK 0-24
Munster SHC Final
Páirc Uí Chaoimh
JULY 13, 2014

Anthony Nash celebrates with his teammates as Cork raise the Munster trophy in 2014, and the old Páirc Úi Chaoimh receives a rousing goodbye.

★ **CORK: A Nash (0-1)**; C Joyce, S O'Neill, S McDonnell; L McLoughlin, M Ellis, D Cahalane; D Kearney, A Walsh (0-2); S Harnedy (1-2), B Cooper (0-2), C Lehane (0-5); A Cadogan (0-3), P Cronin, P Horgan (0-8). Subs: P O'Sullivan (1-1) for Cronin, W Egan for Cahalane, S Moylan for Cadogan.

★ **LIMERICK:** N Quaid; S Hickey, R McCarthy, T Condon; P O'Brien (0-1), W McNamara (0-1), G O'Mahony; J Ryan (0-1), P Browne (0-1); D Breen (0-1), D O'Grady (0-2), D Hannon (0-1); G Mulcahy (0-3), S Dowling (0-12), K Downes (0-1). Subs: S Walsh for O'Brien, S Tobin for Hannon, C King for O'Mahony, T Ryan for Downes.

THE ACTION

IN A GAME that was level on eight occasions – six times in the second-half – goals were always going to be crucial and so it proved, as the Rebels reversed the outcome of the 2013 decider in the Gaelic Grounds. Despite two early misses from placed balls from Shane Dowling, Limerick settled the better, with points from Dowling, James Ryan and Graeme Mulcahy the only scores of the game's opening 10 minutes as Cork laboured.

While Aidan Walsh opened the hosts' account with a smart score after latching onto a break, Limerick remained on top and by the 21st minute it was 0-8 to 0-4 for the visitors.

Conor Lehane was one of the brighter spots in the Cork attack, and he was central to an unanswered seven-point burst as the home team forged ahead for the first time. In keeping with the frenetic nature of the game, however, Limerick were level at half-time at 0-12 each as Paudie O'Brien, Mulcahy, Paul Browne and Dowling all pointed, with Lehane getting Cork's only response.

The opening stages of the second-half were of a similar vein as the sides were level at 0-13, 0-14, 0-16, 0-17 and 0-18 each, with Limerick's opening of a two-point lead quickly eradicated. Dowling and Lehane remained to the fore for their respective sides during this period before the game turned in the 54th minute. With the sides tied, Browne looked to have put Limerick ahead only for his shot to be waved wide and, with the very next attack, Cork had a goal as the Limerick defence opened up, allowing Harnedy to fire past Nickie Quaid from close range.

Limerick centre-back Wayne McNamara replied with a booming effort and, after Horgan scored from the resultant puckout, it took another brilliant defensive flick by O'Neill to stop Browne manoeuvring himself into a goalscoring position.

Bill Cooper profited from the Cork attack that developed after that to put four between the sides, but two from Dowling – one a free – left two in it with eight minutes of normal time left.

Harnedy's second point answered that and then Cork assured themselves of the win as Daniel Kearney dispossessed Séamus Hickey, before sending the ball into half-time sub O'Sullivan and he finished with aplomb.

★★★★★

66

IT'S NICE TO be able to say that I got to play in the last big game in Páirc Uí Chaoimh… and the fact that it was a Munster final.

The year before, we had lost to Limerick at the same stage in the Gaelic Grounds and I remember walking off the field that day and seeing the Limerick supporters embrace their players on their home patch.

I'm a big believer in the provincial championships and a Munster medal was something I wanted to have. It was such a special occasion, especially for a team that had been together and gone so close in 2013.

It just all came together and it was an unbelievable experience.

I played minor for Cork – but in football rather than hurling!

I was on the minor hurling panel for two years but I never played in the championship. The first year, I was sub to Martin Coleman when we won the All-Ireland in 2001, and the second year Shay Bowen came in and he was captain as Erin's Own had won the county championship.

In the football, I played against Waterford, Kerry and Clare, but hurling was always going to be the long-term choice.

I played under-21 in 2005 and we won a Munster title but lost to Galway in the All-Ireland semi-final. I played intermediate for Cork for a few years as well. People often ask me about that competition and I always say I'm hugely in favour of it because, without it, I would never have played for Cork at senior level.

In the winter of 2005, I got the phone call to come in to the senior panel, as Paul Morrissey from Newtownshandrum, the third-choice keeper, had stepped away. It was dream-come-true stuff.

The first training I went to was in Castlemartyr and Brian Corcoran and Seán Óg were walking in at the same time. I wouldn't have known too many of the lads – Kevin Hartnett was the only other fella from that under-21 team who was on the panel – and Corcoran and Seán Óg came over and shook my hand.

Having two of my heroes do that was brilliant.

We got to the All-Ireland final in 2006 and that was a good experience even though I didn't play. Then in 2007, Semplegate happened, Dónal Óg Cusack was suspended and it was going to be either myself or Martin chosen for the Waterford game.

There was no decision made up until the week of the game, no tipping off that either of us was going to get the call or anything, but you could physically feel them watching us closer. I assumed that it was going to be Martin as he was older, but I got the nod.

Obviously, five goals went in that day, but it gave me the experience for later on in life when I got my second chance. I couldn't get over the pace of the game, I'd never experienced anything like it.

So, even though we were beaten, I'd put it down as a positive experience.

The next opportunity came in 2012, after Dónal Óg had been injured in the league semi-final against Tipp. I came on for him that day but Martin was chosen for the final against Kilkenny.

We were down to play Tipp in the first championship match and Jimmy pulled me aside coming into that game. I had trained well beforehand; I did what I'd normally do. He gave me the nod a few weeks before the match; we had a challenge match and he said, 'Look, go and enjoy yourself, you're going to be wearing the No 1 jersey for Cork!'

It gave me a sense of nervousness but there was relief as well that Jimmy had faith in me to go and play championship for Cork. In fairness to Ger and the lads, they all worked around me and helped me prepare.

There was one challenge match where they tried to ruffle my feathers, trying to prepare me for what they thought might happen!

I knew the situation. I was replacing at the time probably the most influential goalkeeper in the game. Against Tipperary that day, we obviously didn't win but there was a sense of... relief is the wrong word, but a huge weight off my shoulders in that I had played for Cork again after such a long wait.

I had won three or four All-Ireland intermediate medals and a Munster under-21 medal but none of that could prepare you for senior championship pace. I used to only get one league game a year and, with no disrespect, it was usually against the weakest team.

Dónal Óg was there to help me and then, later on in the year, when we got to the All-Ireland semi-final against Galway, he drove me up to Dublin to watch a football game in Croke Park. We sat where the referees' supervisors sat, so I could see the whole of the stadium and how big it was.

To be fair, he was great if I wanted anything from him and you have to understand too that it was difficult for him; he had been named as captain that year and then he had to watch another guy come in.

He couldn't have been any more generous to me.

I wasn't always a goalkeeper – at my own age-group, I would have played outfield for Kanturk. I remember we played an under-12 blitz in Ballyhea once and I got some kind of record score, the papers did a thing on me. Next thing, all of a sudden Kanturk had a goalkeeping issue at under-14 and I was called up.

The first time I played in goal, I let in 10 or 12 goals, but I stuck at it!

A cousin on my mam's side would have played in goal for South Liberties as well but all of the Nashes played outfield. I don't know was it just in me or what, but it just worked out that way.

I always wondered if I'd have had the ability to play outfield – I played full-forward for CIT in the Fitzgibbon and I always had a grá for it.

We made it to the All-Ireland semi-finals through the back door in 2012 and I ended up winning an All-Star. If you'd told me in March or April of that year that I'd have got a game in goal for Cork, I'd have snapped your hand off, so to be walking up on stage to collect an award was unbelievable.

I managed to be selected in 2013 too and the two of them are in a room at home because they're my family's, they're not just mine.

My family were up at the All Stars and they were very proud when I won them and it just meant a lot for me to be able to say thanks for driving me around the country and everything else.

Looking back, 2013 was the one that got away.

Ourselves and Clare were two surprise teams in the final. The first day, I thought we had it when 'Hoggy' put the ball over the bar, but it wasn't to be. In 2014, people probably thought that it would be hard for us to come back.

Winning Munster was great for us but the gap between the Munster final and the All-Ireland semi-final didn't help us.

Tipperary were far superior to us on the day and it was disappointing because we felt we'd proven ourselves to not be one-hit wonders, making the All-Ireland final and then winning Munster.

It was a pity. If there was one game that you wish you could have back and do differently, that would be it.

There was a bit of talk beforehand that the Páirc wouldn't be an acceptable venue for Limerick as it was nearing the end of its life and mightn't have been up to scratch, but that wasn't an issue in our camp at all.

To be fair, Jimmy was meticulous about things like that not seeping through to the players. He made you feel 10 feet tall going on to the field and anything that was nonsense or he felt wasn't important, he didn't do... and we didn't deal with it.

We were solely focused on playing in Páirc Uí Chaoimh at that time and we were looking forward to it.

I would get very nervous on the bus to games.

As a goalkeeper, if I dropped a ball it could cost Cork the game, whereas a corner-forward could drop a ball but he'd get another one and have a chance to recover.

Once the ball was thrown in then, you didn't have time to think, or have nerves or anything like that... I just got on with it. If you talk to any players, I don't know if we actually enjoy championship matches, or enjoy the build-up to them anyway.

I used to always sit with Brian Murphy on the bus because he used to calm me down! That was my only real ritual. I was a stickler for having the same gear alright for every game – the same shorts, the same socks, the same boots, but that was because I felt comfortable in them rather than any superstition.

I didn't want to risk trying something new.

Even something like inside-shorts, I always kept a pair just for matches and made sure they were ready. The same if I ever wore a top inside the jersey.

I remember there was a book brought out by *Balls.ie* and they had an article saying that having the socks up was a Cork goalkeeper thing – Martin Coleman, Ger Cunningham and Dónal Óg Cusack all did it – but that was more coincidence than anything.

I just did it as a young fella – I never liked having my socks down because you have to understand, when I was growing up, when they were down around your ankles they were nearly going out over the boot!

I played in goal in soccer too and it was a rule there to have them up, so I just got used to taping them up.

We always sat in the same seats in the dressing-room. When the Páirc was built in the 70s, there were four dressing-rooms but they were fairly small and by the 2000s the teams for the main match used two each, and there were prefabs for the curtain-raiser out the back. I always sat just inside the door of the second dressing-room and Hoggy used to sit across from me.

Whenever Jimmy wanted us, we all went into the main one, the one on the right as you walked in. We were just so used to being inside there... you didn't take any notice of it but it's funny to look back and compare them to what's there now in the new stadium.

Back then, for the warm-up it was about catching and shot-stopping, but the puckouts became more important so I used to make sure my eye was in for striking.

I would never have warmed up too heavily, it was mainly just making sure that I was confident in my touch. If it went well, I'd be happy to cut the warm-up short and go with it. After the national anthem, you'd do a bit of a sprint to get the blood flowing again. A couple of jumps... into the goal and off you go, hoping to God it goes okay.

When I was in my first year minor, 16 years of age, John Considine was the manager and we played Wexford in a challenge match up the country.

I played the first-half and we were against the wind – my puckouts when I was 16 couldn't reach the halfway line. Shay Bowen came on for the second-half and his puckouts were way longer.

John Considine said to me, 'I told you to work on your puckouts for the last few months and you haven't'. I said that I had... I'd bought three or four different hurleys and I just couldn't improve.

He was threatening to drop me off the panel, so my father got in contact with Pat Curran, Ronan's father, whom he had worked with as a garda, and asked if Ronan or someone could help me. Pat said he'd get on to Ger Cunningham...

and he did a lot of work with me on the third pitch at St Finbarr's.

He gave me one of his older hurleys to try out, a longer hurley for puckouts, and showed me a few things with technique and striking. Then, with time, as I got older, gym training became more important and strength training came into it, so my puckouts developed a little bit further again.

But at the time, it was down to Ger improving my technique.

It was hot day for the 2014 final.

I had my head shaved and we were all sweating bricks.

All of the Munster finals I played in were roasting days. We were surrounded by the people in the crowd. I felt that day like I could hardly breathe.

I'd never experienced it before; it was the first big day for me in the stadium. It's impossible to communicate in a packed stadium. It was more visual than vocal when it came to big days. If you're trying to tell a corner-back to go when a fella is bearing down on goal, that's when a crowd is at its loudest… so he's not going to hear you.

The place was thronged.

We were in Division 2 of the league that year because we had been relegated in 2013. The whole year was kind of put into that one game – we almost didn't know it at the time. All of my memories of that day revolve around the crowd.

A lot of games, for me, were just blurs and still are.

I could be playing a club game and you'd ask me about something that happened, and I'd have to watch it back. I've never watched games back unless I've had to break it down.

I never used to watch *The Sunday Game* when I played, but we were out after the game that night – I can't even remember what pub – and it was on.

Dónal Óg was analysing and he picked out a free from my own '45' that I had put over the bar as one of the most important parts of the game. If a goalkeeper makes a save, fantastic, but for me, it felt good to have contributed a big moment.

The goals were obviously the key. It was always nip and tuck and the stand-out moment for me was the relief and the feeling… the elation for Paudie, when he came on and got his goal.

He broke his leg in 2013 and he was gone for the year, which was huge for us.

In the league that year, he was playing centre-forward and he was phenomenal, he was absolutely awesome. We were training inside in CIT and we got the news that he had got injured playing for Imokilly and we were all gutted.

He was one of our leaders. It was fairytale stuff for him to come on and get the goal. The whistle went not long after that and it was mayhem.

It was almost claustrophobic as the crowd came in on top of us; it was just a feeling that I'd never, ever experienced before.

It was enjoyment and relief.

It was brilliant and it's something that I think is missed in the GAA nowadays. It's something that players may never experience again at an inter-county game.

Richie Mooney used to be doing the gear for us and I'd him fairly well warned to come in for my stuff straightaway. I didn't care if all of my sliothars were taken, but I'd be fairly weird about my hurleys… they had to be safe!

We had lost to Limerick the year before; we had lost the All-Ireland final and it was the last game in Páirc Uí Chaoimh, so to win was hugely important.

If we had lost, it would have been another final we hadn't won.

It was my first piece of silverware as a player. I had been a sub when we won Munster in 2006 and it was a great occasion and everything but, as a player, it was my first time being on the field and actually winning something.

We won Munster again in 2017 and '18 and we were as elated, but just the fact that this was in Páirc Uí Chaoimh made it that bit more special.

The dressing-room afterwards was unbelievable and that's the best time.

You come in and you meet everyone and you hug them. Pat Keane was inside there and Briain Hurley, guys who I'd done so much work with.

You're having a laugh and a joke and pictures taken, and all that kind of craic. They're the moments in the GAA that, whenever I decide I'm finished with playing and coaching, are irreplaceable.

They're the key moments in my life, memories that you cherish forevermore. Unfortunately in sport, you probably have more dressing-rooms with the other feeling, than with winning experiences, and that's what makes the good days sweeter.

99

DANIEL KEARNEY

CORK 1-26 LIMERICK 1-19
Munster SHC
LIT Gaelic Grounds
MAY 19, 2019

Daniel Kearney gets his shot off despite the presence of Limerick's William O'Donoghue in the Gaelic Grounds in 2019.

★ **CORK:** A Nash; S O'Donoghue, E Cadogan, N O'Leary; M Coleman, M Ellis, R Downey; B Cooper, D Fitzgibbon (0-1); **D Kearney (0-4)**, S Harnedy (0-4), L Meade (0-2); A Walsh, P Horgan (1-9), C Lehane (0-1). Subs: A Cadogan (0-3) for Lehane, S McDonnell for O'Donoghue, C Joyce for Downey, S Kingston for Meade, D Dalton (0-2) for Walsh.

★ **LIMERICK:** N Quaid; S Finn, M Casey, R English; D Byrnes (0-2), D Hannon, D Morrissey; C Lynch, D O'Donovan; G Hegarty, K Hayes (0-1), T Morrissey (0-1); P Casey, A Gillane (0-9), G Mulcahy (1-4). Subs: S Flanagan for Casey, S Dowling (0-2) for Hegarty, B Murphy for Mulcahy, W O'Donoghue for O'Donovan, D Dempsey for Gillane.

THE ACTION

IN A SENSE, there was a dual purpose to this inspirational Cork victory. In 2018, John Meyler's side had been denied a place in the All-Ireland final as Limerick produced a semi-final fightback at Croke Park; then, the opening game of the 2019 Munster SHC round-robin had seen them well beaten by Tipperary at Páirc Uí Chaoimh. They travelled to Limerick to face the All-Ireland champions knowing that there was little room for error.

In the wake of the Tipp defeat, the management made some big calls. Mark Ellis returned to the side at centre-back, having not been part of the matchday panel for the opening game, while Robert Downey was given his debut at right half-back and Aidan Walsh came into the full-forward line.

In the first-half, Cork lost Conor Lehane to injury in the process of scoring a point but Alan Cadogan, who missed all of 2018 through injury, was a more-than-adequate replacement. Limerick looked to have hit their stride as they led 0-7 to 0-5 inside 14 minutes and though Cork drew level at 0-8 each thanks to Patrick Horgan's fourth point, Limerick pushed on against as Declan Hannon's pass found Graeme Mulcahy and he finished to the net from a tight angle.

Cork could have responded immediately, as Séamus Harnedy exchanged passes with Walsh but Nickie Quaid denied him and, with Horgan uncharacteristically inaccurate from two frees as half-time approached, Limerick were able to take that two-point lead in at the break.

However, Cork were level within four minutes thanks to Luke Meade and Cadogan. While Gillane put Limerick 1-12 to 0-14 ahead, it was the last time the hosts led, with Eoin Cadogan, Niall O'Leary, Mark Coleman and debutant Downey all excelling in defence for Cork.

Two from Horgan had Cork ahead again, with Mulcahy levelling before Daniel Kearney had two in-a-row for Cork. A goal from Horgan – just after a squandered Limerick chance – put them firmly in control, though with six minutes remaining and Cork six ahead, a monumental hook from the excellent Darragh Fitzgibbon denied Cian Lynch a goal chance. From there, Cork wouldn't be denied and were up and running with a seven-point victory.

★★★★★

66

IN 2018, WE won the Munster Championship and progressed to the All-Ireland semi-final, where we met Limerick. Late in the second-half, we were up by six points but then Limerick got a point and another and another… and kept scoring.

They actually led in injury-time, before Patrick Horgan equalised to force extra-time, but Limerick were stronger and won by 3-32 to 2-31 after the 90 minutes.

They went on to win the All-Ireland and we were left with our regrets.

After losing to Tipperary in the first game in the 2019 Munster Championship, our next match was away to Limerick and we had a few reasons to want to do well.

I don't think I ever had the belief that I could play for Cork.

I just liked hurling – my dad was a massive fan and we'd a good club below in Sarsfields. It was only when Jimmy Barry-Murphy saw something in me in 2012 – in a game where I felt I mightn't have even played well – that I was added to the Cork senior panel.

I never played minor for Cork.

When I was a year below the age for under-21 – 2009 – I was on the Cork panel but I was dropped for the championship game. The following year, I was playing. We hammered Waterford in the Munster quarter-final and played Tipperary – the great Tipp team that had all the Mahers and drove them on to win that year's senior All-Ireland – in the semi-final down in Páirc Uí Chaoimh.

We lost by two points after extra-time – we led for a lot of the game but Séamus Hennessy got an important goal for them and the goals were the difference because they won by 2-17 to 0-21. I suppose that gave myself and a lot of other Cork players – the likes of Luke O'Farrell and William Egan – confidence that we could play against the best for the years that were to follow.

I had coaches in Sars like Bertie Óg Murphy, who gave me a chance when I was 17, and Johnny Crowley, who showed a lot of confidence in me when I was a minor. Then, other coaches like Pat Ryan were great too.

But, even with the confidence that they instilled, I don't think I was ever believing in myself enough to play for Cork. I had success at underage with Sars and I was a young senior, but I still didn't think that I had that X-factor to play inter-county.

Jimmy saw something in me, maybe when a lot of other people mightn't have. I think when he was picking the panel in 2012 and '13, it was around speed.

It was only from getting called up to the panel – maybe when I didn't think I deserved to be, I still felt I got lucky – and then playing good challenge games against Clare and Dublin in the summer of 2012, that I felt I settled. I was playing alongside guys like Seán Óg Ó hAilpín and John Gardiner and it was easy to play well around players with a lot of experience.

That gave me massive confidence; that I could actually play at that level, and that moved me to a new platform of maybe where I thought I could do it. I kind of believed in myself a bit and that mindset piece flipped then, in terms of realising your potential... and the self-doubt changes to confidence.

You start controlling games and telling fellas where to go; you start showing leadership skills and that all brings more confidence. It wasn't one moment, but it was just getting the chance to be on the panel, playing a good game or two... getting the chance to come on as a sub in the Munster Championship against Tipperary in 2012... starting against Waterford... to come on in an All-Ireland semi-final.

Then, the real move came for me in 2013.

I got Man of the Match in a game. That was the big break, to start in a Munster Championship game and be influential.

I said... *Right, I'm here!*

What's funny about that type of environment is that you're not going to play well in every game – you'll have good matches and bad matches and okay matches.

It's just about having that kind of resilience and belief. It's like a professional golfer in that you know you're not going to win every tournament – you're actually going to lose ninety or ninety-five percent.

It's similar in most sports – in inter-county hurling, so many championship matches are close to 50-50 beforehand and you're going to play well as often as you play poorly.

If right is right and everything is equal and it's a competitive environment, your performances should be very mixed because you're up against a guy of equal measure, trying to keep you down and play as well as you.

It's about having those moments of realising your potential when you're on top and then to look back and say... *I've played some good games, there were moments where I owned the game and felt totally in control.* Then, obviously, there are moments where, no matter what you do or how hard you try, the ball is just never going to break your way and you get subbed before half-time.

That's happened me in the Munster Championship and I've seen both sides of it, and that's just sport. It's about how you bounce back from the low points, dust yourself down and go again – that's the real measure of a sportsman, rather than how you react or respond in victory.

We had a young enough team – there was Christopher Joyce, myself, Séamus Harnedy all coming in – and on the week of the game, Pa Cronin and Lorcán McLoughlin, who would have been two of our more experienced guys, both got injured.

There were a lot of things not going our way and Clare comprehensively beat us in extra-time in the relegation play-off... and we were going back up to the Gaelic Grounds.

It wasn't really pointing in our favour, but Jimmy had fellas going well and the confidence was relatively high, despite the results leading up to it. He had given guys like myself, Séamie and Darren Sweetnam our chances and another coach mightn't have done that.

He was giving opportunities to players before they were lighting up club championships; it was more that he was unearthing their potential rather than jumping on the back of strong displays.

I think Jimmy was very good at seeing the potential before it was realised, and then giving the confidence to realise it. That's not common, bringing in fellas who mightn't have played minor. Jimmy was able to look beyond that and see something else.

In 2014, we were going really well – we beat Waterford, Clare and Limerick to win Munster so that was a long route home, especially when you consider that we had beaten the All-Ireland champions on the way. It had given us huge confidence, but that long lay-off allowed a bit of complacency to set in and there were definitely huge learnings from that Tipperary game.

I think then in 2015 and '16, the game was really beginning to transform.

Waterford implemented a sweeper game and the traditional Cork game was to get the ball in low and quick, so I think it took us a year or two to get up to speed with that. Once we did, we had two good years in Munster again, but without ever getting to the holy grail of winning the All-Ireland.

We were going into 2019 with an eight-game unbeaten record in the Munster Championship – we played three games to win the last knockout one (or what we thought was the last, until Covid-19's impact) in 2017 and then five in the first round-robin version in 2018. Our first game was against Tipperary in a packed Páirc Uí Chaoimh and we were very confident but those kinds of matches are always all to play for.

Tipperary had regrouped and brought back Liam Sheedy as manager, and they were of a good age and they had good experience. They were very hungry and they just blew us out of the water, really. The really good teams are able to maintain their hunger and professionalism, keep it always high and never let that guard down.

But Munster Championship games were always considered fairly even beforehand. I don't think I ever went into one thinking… *We're definitely going to win here.*

The fans might have a different perception but, as a player, you know there's never going to be anything in it. If you're even five percent off, that'll have a huge effect.

We had played very poorly in the first 15 or 20 minutes and we were only a point or two behind, but you could sense that they were on it a bit more than we were. Then they got that run on us in the third quarter, and our confidence dipped then.

Tipp had the hunger and a new agenda and a point to prove after poor years in 2017 and '18. They hadn't even got out of the group in the first year of the round-robin so they were bound to be disappointed. We took the brunt of their frustrations and that was a tough lesson, especially in your own backyard.

In the old back door system, there might have been a few weeks to regroup before the qualifier match after losing in Munster, but in the round-robin you just had to dust yourself down to go again – and I think that there are positives and negatives to that, but the good outweighs the bad.

You have to decompress straightaway and rebuilding the confidence, individually and as a group, can be very hard. Then, at the same time, that challenge gives you the opportunity to make wrongs right and use the next match as a chance to prove yourself.

That's what's brilliant about the new system.

I remember that week, going to Brookfield, down by UCC, where we used to do our recovery – physical but also mental in terms of recapping the game.

We were back in on the Monday to do the pool-work and the stretching, making sure the bodies were right to go again the following week, and then there was the breaking down of the Tipp game to allow us to go straight into planning for Limerick.

You're up against two different styles and the way you set up and implement your plan is going to be different – the same with match-ups and man-marking. It's all very quick and urgent but maybe there's a value in not being able to give them so much time and so much respect; sometimes, you've too much time to focus on the opposition and that can be a bad thing. You've all that type of stuff at play.

With the turnaround, there's no time to be killing fellas' confidence – it's the opposite, you need to be building fellas up, and that's where the dynamic of a good management team comes in... John Meyler, Kieran Murphy and Donal O'Mahony, fellas who had been around the block and done it before.

Their skills kick in, in terms of how to get players to bounce back, get the confidence up and produce the optimal performance next time.

When I started off with Cork, I played most of my hurling in midfield but by this stage I was operating as a half-forward and that was all related to how the game had changed. As Waterford started with that sweeper system, every team developed and evolved around it. Under Kieran Kingston in 2017, Cork started to take advantage of that new way of playing and in 2018 John gave me the chance to play on the wing in a challenge game against Offaly. I did well and he stuck with me for the Munster Championship.

I played well in the first match against Clare and it just rolled from there.

Séamie Harnedy and Conor Lehane were playing in the half-forward line with me, so I could rely on their strength in the air, and I could withdraw as that third midfielder.

You need that balance – you couldn't have three Daniel Kearneys in the half-forward line! There's an inter-dependency in how the lines interact.

Myself, Séamie and Conor used to talk a lot about keeping the depth – you could just withdraw the whole half-forward line but then you've no platform to attack when you turn over the ball, and it leaves four defenders against two attackers.

There's a lot of teamwork and balance required.

I liked playing in the Gaelic Grounds.

Like Páirc Uí Chaoimh and Thurles, when it was full for a Munster Championship game there was always a great atmosphere and you feed off that.

Limerick hadn't played in the first round of fixtures, so this was their first championship match as All-Ireland champions. There was expectation and pressure on them as well and, to be fair, they didn't have a bad game but I think we really played to our full strengths.

From the first ball right to the last minute, it was a complete performance and everyone contributed.

I was being marked by Diarmaid Byrnes, but when you're moving so much and with the way Limerick play, it's more about zones – you're nearly on midfielders and other half-backs as much as the fella you walk over to at the throw-in.

I ended up with four points from play. Aidan Walsh was coming out as a disruptive half-forward and I was moving into his area. We were just playing really well as a team, with good movement and good inter-play.

I scored more later in my career, but I think a lot of it was down to the game developing. If you take Limerick as an example, their half-back line played zonally so it gave me that opportunity to be a bit freer. Our full-forward line was picked up and they had half-backs sweeping as well as trying to watch their own men.

That meant someone like Hoggy maybe wasn't getting as much clean ball into him, but it gave me more opportunity out the field. It was more an effect of the game developing rather than me becoming any bit more accurate.

When you play with Cork, there's a lot of pride that comes with the jersey and you're always aware of the responsibility that you have and your ability to impact people's moods around the county. When you lose and play poorly, you carry that sense of hurt and pain and you want to make it right.

That day, we did that.

What was disappointing was that, after the Limerick game, we had a poor performance against Waterford, though we still did the job.

Then we went to play Clare in Ennis in the final match and it was a dog's dinner of a game but, again, you're playing a team that's every bit as good as you and is running every bit as hard as you. If you're just that bit off, things don't go your way.

We got out of Munster and beat Westmeath, but that Kilkenny game in the quarter-final… we had chances to build a lead in the first-half but we never took them and they blew us out of it in the third quarter.

I remember reading Richie McCaw say that what he missed most after retirement were the moments after a game in the dressing-room with the group, and it's true of sport at all levels. Winning a game where your backs are against the wall is something you treasure… that sense of camaraderie and achievement where you play to your potential and put in a performance.

Then, when you exit the stadium, you're on to the next day.

You're trying to take the confidence from the result but remove the complacency that comes with winning. Sometimes, finding that balance can be tricky, but the memories of a win like that one over Limerick stay with you.

COMING
IN
2022

THREE MORE BOOKS

WHERE CORK GAA STARS REVISIT THE DAY THAT
DEFINED THEIR LIVES...

www.**HERO**BOOKS.digital

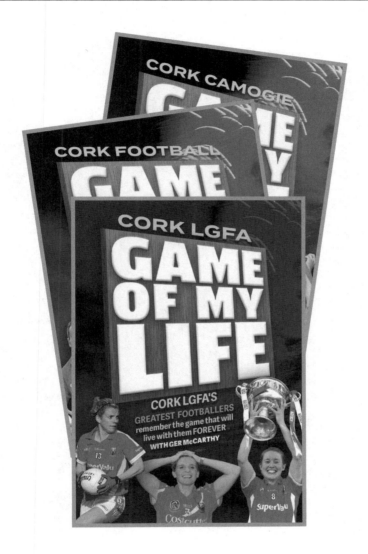

CORK LGFA ★ APRIL 2022

CORK CAMOGIE ★ SEPTEMBER 2022

CORK FOOTBALL ★ OCTOBER 2022

MORE
GREAT

BOOKS FROM
HEROBOOKS

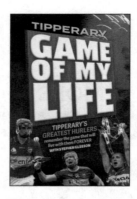

TIPPERARY
GAME OF MY LIFE

THE GREATEST TIPPERARY hurlers over the last 50 years remember the one game in blue and gold that defined their lives...

Including: Jimmy Finn, Theo English, Tony Wall, Tadhg O'Connor, Dinny Ryan, Babs Keating, John Sheedy, Ken Hogan, Colm Bonnar, Cormac Bonnar, Declan Carr, Michael Cleary, Pat Fox, Conal Bonnar, Declan Ryan, Michael Ryan, Joe Hayes, Eamonn Corcoran, Tommy Dunne, Shane McGrath, James Woodlock, Brendan Cummins, Eoin Kelly, Michael Cahill, Brendan Maher, James Barry, Seamus Callinan and more...

A game that will live with each man forever.

Author: Stephen Gleeson
Hardback: €25.00
Paperback: €20.00
Ebook: €9.99
ISBN: 9781910827185

Buy on **Amazon**
(and paperback available in all good bookstores)

GALWAY
GAME OF MY LIFE

TWENTY-FIVE OF GALWAY'S greatest hurlers remember the one game that will live with them forever...

Including: Jimmy Hegarty, Ned Dervan, Andy Fenton, Iggy Clarke, Sean Silke, Joe Connolly, PJ Molloy, Noel Lane, John Connolly, Mike Conneely, Anthony Cunningham, Pete Finnerty, Eanna Ryan, Gerry McInerney, John Commins, Michael Coleman, Micheál Donoghue, Padraig Kelly, Kevin Broderick, Ger Farragher, David Collins, Ollie Canning, Alan Kerins, Fergal Moore and Gearoid McInerney.

The day that defined their lives...

Author: Ollie Turner
Hardback: €25.00
Paperback: €20.00
Ebook: €9.99
ISBN: 9781910827284

Buy on **Amazon**
(and paperback available in all good bookstores)

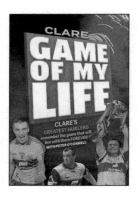

CLARE
GAME OF MY LIFE

30 OF THE GREATEST CLARE hurlers over the last 60 years remember the one game in their careers that defined their sporting lives.

Including: Naoise Jordan, Jackie O'Gorman, Seamus Durack, Sean O'Hehir, Colm Honan, Sean Stack, Tommy Keane, Tommy Guilfoyle, David Forde, Ollie Baker, Stephen McNamara, Frank Lohan, Fergie Tuohy, Gerry McInerney, Fergal Hegarty, Ger Loughnane, Niall Gilligan, Gerry Quinn, Anthony Daly, Brian O'Connell, Fergal Lynch, Cian Dillon, Podge Collins, Brendan Bugler, Pat O'Connor, Colin Ryan, Patrick Donnellan, Conor Ryan, John Conlon and Tony Kelly

A game that will live with each man forever.

Author: Peter O'Connell
Hardback: €25.00
Paperback: €20.00
Ebook: €9.99
ISBN: 9781910827376

Buy on **Amazon**
(and paperback available in all good bookstores)

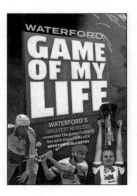

WATERFORD
GAME OF MY LIFE

25 OF THE GREATEST WATERFORD hurlers over the last 60 years remember the one game in their careers that defined their sporting lives.

Including: Tom Cunningham, Martin Óg Morrissey, Michael O'Connor, Larry Guinan, Jim Greene, Brian Greene, Patricia Jackman, Mossie Walsh, John Galvin, Shane Ahearne, Stephen Frampton, Fergal Hartley, Sean Cullinane, Brian Flannery, Eoin Murphy, John Mullane, Beth Carton , Paul Flynn , Dan Shanahan and Maurice Shanahan

A game that will live with each person forever.

Author: Tómas McCarthy
Hardback: €25.00
Paperback: €20.00
Ebook: €9.99
ISBN: 9781910827406

Buy on **Amazon**
(and paperback available in all good bookstores)

DUBLIN
GAME OF MY LIFE

25 OF THE GREATEST DUBLIN footballers over the last 60 years remember the one game in their careers that defined their sporting lives.

Including: Jim Crowley, Bernard Brogan Snr, Paddy Cullen, Tommy Drumm, Tommy Conroy, Gerry Hargan, Johnny Magee, Paddy Christie, Paul Curran, Vinnie Murphy, Kevin Nolan, Charlie Redmond, Paul Griffin, Ray Cosgrove, John O'Leary, Barney Rock, Kieran Duff, Jack Sheedy, Alan Larkin, Robbie Kelleher, Shane Ryan, Ger Brennan, Tommy Carr, Ciarán Whelan, Collie Moran and Alan Brogan

A game that will live with each man forever.

Author: David Sheehan
Hardback: €25.00
Paperback: €20.00
Ebook: €9.99
ISBN: 9781910827383

Buy on **Amazon**
(and paperback available in all good bookstores)

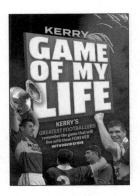

KERRY
GAME OF MY LIFE

30 OF THE GREATEST KERRY footballers over the last 60 years remember the one game in their careers that defined their sporting lives.

Including: Mick O'Dwyer, Sean Murphy, Michael Gleeson, Ger O'Keeffe, Ger Power, Mickey Ned O'Sullivan, John O'Keeffe, Paudie O'Mahoney, Sean Walsh, Eoin Liston, Mikey Sheehy, Jimmy Deenihan, Ambrose O'Donovan, Tommy Doyle, Jack O'Shea, Billy O'Shea, Dara O'Cinneide, Darragh O Se, Tomas O Se, Seamus Moynihan, Mike Frank Russell, Sean O'Sullivan, Eoin Brosnan, Marc O Se, Killian Young, Darran O'Sullivan, Tom O'Sullivan, Kieran Donaghy, Eamonn Fitzmaurice and Fionn Fitzgerald

A game that will live with each man forever.

Author: David Byrne
Hardback: €25.00
Paperback: €20.00
Ebook: €9.99
ISBN: 9781910827390

Buy on **Amazon**
(and paperback available in all good bookstores)

MEATH
GAME OF MY LIFE

25 OF THE GREATEST MEATH footballers over the last 60 years remember the one game in their careers that defined their sporting lives.

Including: Peter Darby, Jack Quinn, Mattie Kerrigan, Sean Boylan, Colm Coyle, Liam Hayes, Bob O'Malley David Beggy, Colm O'Rourke, Martin O'Connell, Bernard Flynn, Kevin Foley, Finian Murtagh, Tommy Dowd, Trevor Giles, Darren Fay, Graham Geraghty, Jody Devine, Ollie Murphy, Stephen Bray, Anthony Moyles, Kevin Reilly, Joe Sheridan, Mickey Burke and Graham Reilly

A game that will live with each man forever.

Author: Fergal Lynch
Hardback: €25.00
Paperback: €20.00
Ebook: €9.99
ISBN: 9781910827338

Buy on **Amazon**
(and paperback available in all good bookstores)

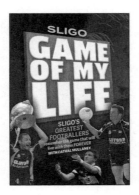

SLIGO
GAME OF MY LIFE

30 OF THE GREATEST SLIGO footballers over the last 60 years remember the one game in their careers that defined their sporting lives.

Including: Noel Mullaney, Micheal Kearins, Liam Caffrey, Brendan McCauley, Jim Colleary, John Brennan, Mattie Brennan, Paddy Henry, Mattie Hoey, Barnes Murphy, Mick Laffey, John Kent, Fintan Feeney, Bernard Mulhern, Tommy Breheny, Paul Taylor, Pat Kilcoyne, Brendan Kilcoyne, Sean Davey, Dessie Sloyan, Paul Durcan, John McPartland, Eamonn O'Hara, Mark Breheny, Noel McGuire, Michael McNamara, David Kelly, Ross Donovan, Adrian Marren and Niall Murphy.

A game that will live with each man forever.

Author: Cathal Mullaney
Hardback: €25.00
Paperback: €20.00
Ebook: €9.99
ISBN: 9781910827321

Buy on **Amazon**
(and paperback available in all good bookstores)

MORE
GREAT
SPORTS BOOKS
FROM
HERO BOOKS

The Pressure Game
Kevin McStay: An Autobiography

FOR THE FIRST time one of the top GAA managers in the country has revealed the inside story of what it's like to 'Walk the Walk on a County Sideline'. Former Mayo Allstar footballer Kevin McStay gave up 20 years of working as a commentator and analyst on RTE's Sunday Game to take up the position of Roscommon team manager in 2016.

The whole country watched to see how he would survive on the sideline – and how he would face up to the pressures of facing Jim's Gavin's Dublin, Mayo and Kerry and Tyrone, on the toughest stage in Gaelic football.

In his three years in charge, McStay led Roscommon to a Connacht title in 2017 and a prized place in the Super 8s in 2018 before quitting the job. He has now returned to the RTE broadcasting booth.

This is the amazing inside story of the **The Pressure Game**.

Authors: Kevin McStay with Liam Hayes
Hardback: €25.00
Paperback: €20.00
Ebook: €9.99
ISBN: 9781910827086

Buy on **Amazon**
(and paperback available in all good bookstores)

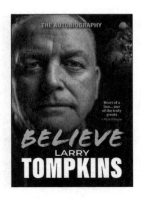

BELIEVE

Larry Tompkins: An Autobiography

HIS SELF-BELIEF WAS unbreakable. His iron will inspirational. Nothing could stop Larry Tompkins. No man, no team, as he made his football life the greatest story ever told in the long and brilliant history of the GAA.

Six years with his native Kildare left him empty-handed and heartbroken. He emigrated to New York to find a job and find a team he could lead to championship glory. In the United States, Tompkins' belief in himself never dimmed. He led Donegal to four New York championships in the Big Apple. He also found a new home for himself in Ireland and led Castlehaven to two Cork and Munster titles. In between, he also became the most valuable and feared footballer in Ireland.

BELIEVE is the story of a man who defied all the odds. In Cork's magnificent red shirt, he led his adopted county to two All-Ireland titles in 1989 and 90, one National League and six Munster titles, and he also was honoured with three All Star awards. Upon his retirement, Larry Tompkins continued to lead and inspire, and make others believe too.

Authors: Larry Tompkins with Denis Hurley
Hardback: €25.00
Paperback: €20.00
Ebook: €9.99
ISBN: 9781910827123

Buy on **Amazon**
(and paperback available in all good bookstores)

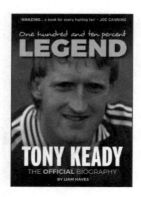

One Hundred and Ten Percent Legend
Tony Keady: The Official Biography

WHEN TONY KEADY died suddenly in August of 2017, at just 53 years of age, a whole county mourned and the rest of the country stopped in its tracks to say goodbye to a legend of the game of hurling.

In 1988, after leading Galway to a second All-Ireland title in succession, he was crowned the greatest hurler in Ireland. He was 25 years of age and there was nobody like him, nobody to touch him in the maroon No.6 shirt. But, four years later, and still not 30, after being wrongly banned for 12 months by the GAA, he was also discarded by his own county and refused a maroon jersey the very last time he walked out onto Croke Park behind the Galway team.

A few months before his death, Tony Keady visited Liam Hayes and told him he wished to tell his own story. He felt it was time, but tragically time was not on Tony's side. Tony's wife Margaret and his daughter Shannon and his three boys Anthony, Harry and Jake, decided to finish telling the story of a father and a hurler who always asked those around him for '110%'.

Author: Liam Hayes
Hardback: €25.00
Paperback: €20.00
Ebook: €9.99
ISBN: 9781910827048

Buy on **Amazon**
(and paperback available in all good bookstores)

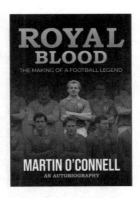

Royal Blood
Martin O'Connell: An Autobiography

THREE TIMES ALL-IRELAND winner, Martin O'Connell was crowned the prince of wing backs in 2000 when he was selected on the GAA's Team of the Millennium, and had a postage stamp issued in his honour. This honour also stamped O'Connell's name down in Meath football history as the greatest of the greats.

As a Meath footballer, O'Connell truly had Royal Blood. He was a central player on Sean Boylan's 1987 and 88 All-Ireland winning teams, and then remained with Boylan to win a third All-Ireland in 1996 in an infamous replayed final against Mayo.

Now, O'Connell reveals the inside story of those battling years, and explains how it might never have happened after he quit the Meath team in the mid 80s. But his love of the game brought him back.

In addition to his three All-Irelands, Martin O'Connell won six Leinster titles and three National league titles and in 1996 was named Footballer of the Year.

Authors: Martin O'Connell and David Sheehan
Hardback: €25.00
Paperback: €20.00
Ebook: €9.99
ISBN: 9781910827109

Buy on **Amazon**
(and paperback available in all good bookstores)

Chiselled from Ash
Len Gaynor: An Autobiography

CHISELLED FROM ASH is a story of love and honour.

It's the story of Len Gaynor's great love for the game of hurling, and how he has honoured the great game his whole life.

Len Gaynor won it all with Tipperary, finishing his career with three All-Ireland hurling titles, four Munster titles and two National League titles in the 1960s and 70s. But the flamboyant wing back also wanted to give back at the end of his career.

The Kilruane MacDonaghs clubman – and winner of three county titles – quickly proved himself to be one of the smartest and most ambitious coaches in the game. At club level he strived to teach and help the next generation, and led his own Kilruane and neighbouring clubs to success – and at county level through the 1990s Len Gaynor managed Tipperary and Clare on the biggest stages in the game.

Authors: Len Gaynor with Shane Brophy
Hardback: €25.00
Paperback: €20.00
Ebook: €9.99
ISBN: 9781910827208

Buy on **Amazon**
(and paperback available in all good bookstores)

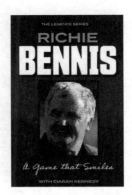

'A Game that Smiles'
The Richie Bennis Autobiography

RICHIE BENNIS IS one of the true legends remaining in the game of hurling. A towering figure in Limerick GAA, he played a central role as the county won the All-Ireland title in 1973 and then he strived as hard as anyone to see the Liam MacCarthy Cup return to the Treaty County.

It was a wait of 45 years – during which time Bennis worked at grassroots hurling in the famed Patrickswell club, where he hurled into his 40s and won 10 county titles. He also led Limerick as team manager to the 2007 All-Ireland final where they lost to Kilkenny.

In 2018, Limerick were crowned All-Ireland champions.

For Richie Bennis, a long agonising wait ended. His story is one of triumph, and heartache and personal tragedy, and a courage that was never dimmed.

Authors: Richie Bennis with Ciarán Kennedy
Hardback: €25.00
Paperback: €20.00
Ebook: €9.99
ISBN: 9781910827093

Buy on **Amazon**
(and paperback available in all good bookstores)

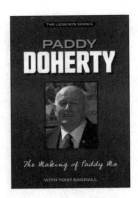

The Making of Paddy Mo
Paddy Doherty: An Autobiography

TO THIS DAY, Down's Paddy Doherty is still remembered as one of the most lethal finishers in the history of Gaelic football. The Ballykinlar clubman was fast, and breathtaking on the ball.

He led his county to a long awaited All-Ireland victory in 1960, and the following summer he captained the Mournemen and brought the Sam Maguire Cup back across the border a second time.

Doherty continued to rip apart defences throughout the decade and won a third All-Ireland crown with Down in 1968, when the Mournemen defeated Kerry in September for the second time, to add to seven Ulster titles and three National league titles.

The 1960s was a decade which is best remembered for the legend of Paddy Doherty.

And... The Making of Paddy Mo.

Authors: Paddy Doherty with Tony Bagnall
Hardback: €25.00
Paperback: €20.00
Ebook: €9.99
ISBN: 9781910827178

Buy on **Amazon**
(and paperback available in all good bookstores)

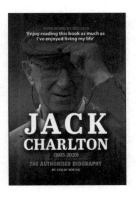

Jack Charlton
The Authorised Biography

AS ONE OF the true legends of Irish and English football, Jack Charlton was a man both loved and feared, but now the people who have lived with him all of his life introduce the real 'Big Jack' in this brilliant authorised biography which is presented in a foreword by Jack himself.

For the first time Jack's wife and family, his teammates as a World Cup winner with England in 1966, and his players during his management years with Middlesbrough, Sheffield Wednesday, Newcastle, and Ireland tell their stories of the man who dominated their lives. Graeme Souness, Chris Waddle, and Peter Beardsley amongst others, are joined by Mick McCarthy, Niall Quinn and the greatest footballers who played under Big Jack for 10 years as Ireland team boss.

This is the most personable, inviting and intimate account of Jack Charlton's life, and the book contains photographs published for the first time from Jack and Pat Charlton's personal collection.

Author: Colin Young
Hardback: €25.00
Paperback: €20.00
Ebook: €9.99
ISBN: 9781910827017

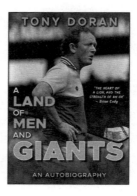

A Land of Men and Giants
The Tony Doran Autobiography

WEXFORD'S ALL-IRELAND winning hero Tony Doran was a giant in the game of hurling through the 1960s, 70s and 80s, at a time when full-forwards were ordered to plunder goals. In his 19 years and 187 appearances as a Wexford hurler, Tony Doran successfully went for goal 131 times. But Doran also played against giants from Kilkenny, Tipperary and Cork, and so many other counties, at a time when the game of hurling tested the wits and the courage of every man on the field.

Some of these men became giants.

A Land of Men and Giants is the story told by Tony Doran of a life spent living and competing against legendary men and true giants of the game.

A Land of Men and Giants: The Autobiography of Tony Doran is edited by award-winning writer and author Liam Hayes.

Authors: Tony Doran with Liam Hayes
Hardback: €25.00
Paperback: €20.00
Ebook: €9.99
ISBN: 9781910827031

Buy on **Amazon**
(and paperback available in all good bookstores)

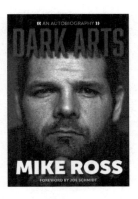

Dark Arts
Mike Ross: An Autobiography

FOR THE FIRST time, Mike Ross brings sports fans into the dark heart of the professional game of rugby union. Ross is recognised as the greatest scrummager in Irish rugby history – and the man who was the foundation stone for the beginning of the Joe Schmidt era, which saw Leinster win back-to-back Heineken Cups and Ireland become the greatest team in Europe.

But Mike Ross might never have been a professional rugby player. He did not turn pro until he was 26 years of age. And he spent three years learning his trade at the toughest end of the game with Harlequins in England before coming home at 30, and chasing the dream of an Irish jersey. Ross would play 61 times for Ireland, and over 150 times for Leinster. His story is one of big dreams and amazing courage, on and off the field. He writes about the good times and the hardest times, facing the true beasts of the professional game every weekend.

Authors: Mike Ross with Liam Hayes
Hardback: €25.00
Paperback: €20.00
Ebook: €9.99
ISBN: 9781910827048

Buy on **Amazon**
(and paperback available in all good bookstores)